DATE			
NOV 3 77			

old french silver

a handbook for the collector

Old French Silver

Wilfred Cripps

NEWBURY BOOKS

First published 1880

This illustrated edition published
in 1972 by the Dolphin Press
Christchurch, Hampshire, England

© by the Dolphin Press

Published in the United States
of America in 1973 by
Newbury Books, 29 Commonwealth
Avenue, Boston 02116 USA

L.C.C. No. 73-78444
SBN 0-912728-01-9

printed in Great Britain

old
french
silver

---

w. cripps

 THE DOLPHIN PRESS CHRISTCHURCH

First published 1880.
This illustrated edition
published 1972 by
The Dolphin Press
176 Barrack Road
Christchurch Hants.

SBN 85642.004.2

Printed in Great Britain
by Megaron Press Ltd
Bournemouth Hants.

Bound by James Burn
at Esher Surrey

CONTENTS.

—◆—

CHAPTER I.

PAGE

French weights and measures—The old marc weight—The modern
metric system—Table for the conversion of Troy weight into
grammes—Table comparing grammes, Troy weight, and marcs
— Coin used as weights—French standards for gold—Value of
gold of different qualities—Standards for silver—Value of various
qualities of silver 1

CHAPTER II.

The early goldsmiths of Limoges—St. Martial and St. Eloi—The
goldsmiths' guild in Paris—Ancient code for their government
—Ordinances of Philippe le Hardi and Philippe le Bel—Letters
of Confirmation of King John—The craft in the Provinces—The
goldsmiths of Montpellier—The Ordinance of 1506—Introduction
of date-letters—The Renaissance of Art—List of goldsmiths of
the sixteenth century—The school of the Louvre—Destruction
of plate under Louis XIV.—Imposition of the droit de marque
—The goldsmiths of the seventeenth century—The plate of the
Regency—The Rococo period—The classical style—The goldsmiths of the eighteenth century—Summary of the marks on old
Paris plate—Table of the Paris date-letters—Table of the marks
of the Farmers-General of the duty   8

CHAPTER III.

Ancient provincial hall-marks—The Mint letters of provincial centres
—The marks of 1783—The standards of Burgundy and Lorraine
—Table of arms of towns where plate was made before 1783—
Table of the marks used under the administration of Jn. Bte.
Fouache, 1774-1780—Table of the town marks used from 1783-
1789 50

CHAPTER IV.

The modern hall-marks of 1791, 1809, 1819, and 1838, with tables . 80

INDEX   97

b

PREFACE.

THE estimation in which old French plate is held, and the high price it therefore commands both in Paris and London, render a knowledge of the hall-marks used in France as desirable and even necessary as an acquaintance with English marks is admitted to be for connoisseurs of old English plate.

The marks placed upon French plate since the Revolution are well known, having been published both in France and in our own country : but whilst these, which are valueless to the collector of old plate, have been often printed, no attempt has been made to interpret the marks by which the date and the maker or at all events the place of manufacture of antique plate, which is of so much greater historical and artistic interest, may usually be identified.

The destruction of French records in troublous times, the difficulty of putting together the fragments that

remain, and the want of opportunity of collating them
with specimens of plate that are not to be found every
day, may possibly be thought a sufficient explanation
of this, as well as an excuse for the mistakes that may
be found in the following pages. Some mistakes must
needs occur when a subject is dealt with for the first
time, and then by a foreigner; but, even allowing for
these, it is believed that the reader will find himself
able, with the aid of the following tables of old Paris
date-letters and fac-similes of the marks used by the
Fermiers-Généraux of the duty, to fix the date of almost
every specimen of old plate made in Paris, and to ascer-
tain the origin of a good deal of the old provincial
French plate that he has an opportunity of examining.

These hitherto unpublished tables, originally con-
structed by the author for his own use, are now printed
at the request of many friends and correspondents; and
any corrections of them, additions to them, or notes of
any kind that may render them more accurate and
complete, would be gladly received by him.

The historical chapter is founded upon the best works
on French gold and silversmiths' work, especially those
of Labarte, Laborde, Lacroix, and Lasteyrie, and the

preface to the catalogue published in 1878 of a portion of the Pichon Collection. The author has endeavoured to condense into it much that, already well said by these writers, has not been hitherto in a handy form for the English collector. For modern hall-marks the best French treatises have been consulted and compared. The author cannot be sufficiently grateful to the Baron Jérôme Pichon and Mr. A. W. Franks for their valued help. To Messrs. Lamberts he is indebted for a table of duty and other marks; and to Mr. Charles Read for the armorial bearings of nearly two hundred French towns.

W. J. C.

CIRENCESTER,
June, 1880.

Silver coffee pot with the mark of J.C. Roquillet-Desnoyers and the Paris mark for 1780-1781. Victoria & Albert Museum.

A

HANDBOOK FOR THE COLLECTOR

OF

OLD FRENCH PLATE.

CHAPTER I.

FRENCH WEIGHTS AND STANDARDS.

French weights and measures—The old marc weight—The modern
metric system—Table for the conversion of Troy weight into
grammes—Table comparing grammes, Troy weight, and marcs—
Coin used as weights—French standards for gold—Value of gold of
different qualities—Standards for silver—Value of various qualities
of silver.

In the Statutes of the Goldsmiths of Paris it is
prescribed that the aspirant for reception into the Guild
as "Maître et Marchand" must be examined by the
six wardens in the divisions of the marc weight, the
prices and qualities of gold and silver wares, and the
mode of alloying base and fine metal so as to raise or
reduce it to the proper standards for working according
to the various ordinances of the craft.

If some of this learning would be profitless to the
amateur, the divisions of the marc weight still have an
interest from an antiquarian point of view; and a comparison of these old weights with the more modern
French, and the English Troy, tables will be found of

practical use, at all events by the purchaser of old French plate.

Enough has been said elsewhere about the alloys of gold and silver and the methods of assaying those metals, but a few preliminary remarks upon the French standards for coin and plate, seem as necessary as some knowledge of French weights. Taking then the above statute for our text, let us devote a page or two first to weights, and then to standards.

TABLE OF OLD FRENCH MARC WEIGHTS.

1 Marc =. 8 ounces = 64 gros = 192 deniers⁻= 4608 grains.
　　1 ounce　= 8 gros = 24 deniers = 576 grains.
　　　　　1 gros = 3 deniers = 72 grains.
　　　　　　　　1 denier = 24 grains.

In the old French royal accounts and inventories of the fifteenth and subsequent centuries, the weight of gold and silver plate is usually given in marcs, ounces, and gros or deniers. In the thirteenth and fourteenth century the ounce was as often divided into 20 *esterlins*.

1360-68. Sis cuillers dor, de plaine euvre, toutes pareilles, sanz différence, pesans 1 marc 11 onces xxd.—*Inventaire du Duc d'Anjou.*

1380. Un hanap d'or, plain, à couvercle, de la façon d'un calice et a un fruitelet d'une roze, pesant ij marcs vi onces v esterlins.— *Inventaire de Charles V.*

1453. Une couppe d'argent dorée dedens et dehors, poinssonné dessus à ung compaignon et une damoiselle, pesant deux marcs trois onces ung gros.—*Acte de vente des biens de Jacques Cœur.*

1506. Quatre tranchoirs d'or dont en y a deux ronds et deux carrés, pesans ensemble x marcs iij onces vii gros.—*Inventaire de la royne Anne de Bretagne.*

The marc weight was abolished at the Revolution, and in 1795 its use was prohibited. The new *gramme* weights of the Metric System, which was then substituted for it, are used throughout in the law of 19 Brumaire, Year VI. (1797); but the equivalents of the gramme weights, according to the old computation, are

added in brackets, the public being as yet unfamiliar
with the new mode of reckoning.

WEIGHTS OF THE METRIC SYSTEM.

1 kilogramme = 10 hectogrammes = 100 décagrammes = 1,000 grammes = 10,000 décigrammes
 1 hectogramme = 10 décagrammes = 100 grammes = 1,000 décigrammes
 1 décagramme = 10 grammes = 100 décigrammes.
 1 gramme = 10 décigrammes.

It will be seen by the following tables of comparison
that the gramme is equivalent to about 19 of the old
French grains, or about 15 grains of Troy weight.

TABLE FOR THE CONVERSION OF TROY WEIGHT INTO GRAMMES.

Troy.		Grammes.	Troy.	Grammes.
1 dwt.		= 1·555	.5 dwt.	= 155·517
5 ,,	(¼ oz.)	= 7·775	6 ,,	= 186·621
10 ,,	(½ oz.)	= 15·551	7 ,,	= 217·724
15 ,,	(¾ oz.)	= 23·327	8 ,,	= 248·828
20 ,,	(1 oz.)	= 31·103	9 ,,	= 279·931
2 oz.		= 62·207	10 ,,	= 311·035
3 ,,		= 93·310	11 ,,	= 342·138
4 ,,		= 124·414	12 ,, (1 lb.)	= 373·242

COMPARATIVE TABLE OF GRAMMES, TROY WEIGHT, AND MARCS.

Grammes.	Troy.					Old French Marcs.			
1 =			15 grains =					19 grains
2 =		1 dwt.	7 ,,	=				38 ,,
3 =		1 ,,	22 ,,	=				56 ,,
4 =		2 ,,	14 ,,	=		1 gros 3 ,,
5 =		3 ,,	5 ,,	=		1 ,, 22 ,,
6 =		3 ,,	21 ,,	=		1 ,, 41 ,,
7 =		4 ,,	12 ,,	=		1 ,, 60 ,,
8 =		5 ,,	3 ,,	=		2 ,, 7 ,,
9 =		5 ,,	19 ,,	=		2 ,, 25 ,,
(1 déca-gramme) 10 =		6 ,,	10 ,,	=		2 ,, 44 ,,
20 =		12 ,,	20 ,,	=		5 ,, 17 ,,
30 =		19 ,,	7 ,,	=		7 ,, 61 ,,
40 =	1 oz. 5 ,,		17 ,,	=		1 oz. 2 ,, 33 ,,
50 =	1 ,, 12 ,,		3 ,,	=		1 ,, 5 ,, 5 ,,
60 =	1 ,, 18 ,,		13 ,,	=		1 ,, 7 ,, 50 ,,
70 =	2 ,, 5 ,,		0 ,,	=		2 ,, 2 ,, 22 ,,
80 =	2 ,, 11 ,,		10 ,,	=		2 ,, 4 ,, 66 ,,
90 =	2 ,, 17 ,,		20 ,,	=		2 ,, 7 ,, 38 ,,

COMPARATIVE TABLE OF GRAMMES, ETC.—*continued.*

	Grammes.			Troy.					Old French Marcs.		
(1 hecto- gramme) }	100 =	3 oz.	4 dwt.	7 grains	=				3 oz.	2 gros	11 grains
	200 =	6 ,,	8 ,,	14 ,,	=			6	,, 4 ,,	21	,,
	300 =	9 ,,	12 ,,	21 ,,	= 1 marc	1	,,	6	,,	32	,,
	400 =	12 ,,	17 ,,	4 ,,	= 1	,,	5	,, 0	,,	43	,,
	500 =	16 ,,	1 ,,	12 ,,	= 2	,,	0	,, 2	,,	54	,,
	600 =	19 ,,	5 ,,	19 ,,	= 2	,,	3	,, 4	,,	64	,,
	700 =	22 ,,	10 ,,	2 ,,	= 2	,,	6	,, 7	,,	3	,,
	800 =	25 ,,	14 ,,	9 ,,	= 3	,,	2	,, 1	,,	14	,,
	900 =	28 ,,	18 ,,	16 ,,	= 3	,,	5	,, 3	,,	24	,,
(1 kilo- gramme) }	1000 =	32 ,,	3 ,,	0 ,,	= 4	,,	0	,, 5	,,	35	,,

It may be added that the French silver franc piece weighs 5 grammes, the 2-franc piece 10 grammes, and the 5-franc piece 25 grammes. The bronze 5-centime piece weighs 5 grammes, and the 10-centime piece 10 grammes. Unworn French coin of such descriptions can, therefore, be used as weights on emergency at these rates.

FRENCH (PARIS) STANDARDS.

GOLD.—Gold is divided into 24 carats, and the carat into 32 grains.

The old French standard for gold plate was $19\frac{1}{5}$ carats, which was called gold "of the touch of Paris," or *or de touche.* This standard is mentioned in the thirteenth, fourteenth, and fifteenth centuries.

In 1554 the standard was raised to 22 carats, with a remedy of a quarter of a carat or 8 grains. It should be remembered that from 1578, 22-carat gold, or, given in millièmes, gold of millesimal fineness ·916.66, has been the English standard for plate, and from 12 Charles II. for coin also.

In 1721 a second quality of gold was allowed to be used for small wares; this was $20\frac{1}{4}$ carats fine, with a remedy of a quarter of a carat.

In 1797 these two standards were abolished by the law so well known as that of 19 Brumaire, Year VI., and the following new ones adopted, which have re-- mained the French standards to the present day :

1st standard = ·920, or $22\frac{5}{64}$ carats, fine.

2nd   ,,   = ·840, or $20\frac{11}{64}$ carats, fine.

3rd   ,,   = ·750, or 18 carats, fine.

A remedy of 3 millièmes is allowed in the case of all these three standards.

In England a second standard of 18 carats was first allowed in 1798, or about the same time as in France.

The French standard for gold coin is ·900, or in French carat measure, 21 carats 19 grains (English 21 carats $2\frac{3}{8}$ grains) fine ; and its value per Troy ounce would be £3 16s. $5\frac{1}{4}d.$, at the English Mint price of 22-carat gold, which is £3 17s. $10\frac{1}{2}d.$ per ounce. This would be, in grammes and French money, 3·0718 francs per gramme.

At the same rate the following intrinsic values per gramme may be given for the three other qualities of French gold that have been mentioned above, viz. :—

·920 = 3·137 francs per gramme.

·840 = 2·867   ,,   ,,

·750 = 2·561   ,,   ,,

Fine gold is worth 3·414 francs per gramme.

SILVER.—The fineness of silver was measured in deniers, oboles and grains : the unit or ounce being divided into 12 deniers, and each denier into 2 oboles or 24 grains.

The earliest recognized standard was English sterling, of 11 deniers $2\frac{2}{5}$ grains fine, or in millièmes ·925. This was the standard in 1260, and no other is mentioned till 1355, when *argent-le-roy* is heard of for the first time. The *argent-le-roy* was 11 deniers 12 grains fine without the solder, for which a remedy of 3 grains in the case of large wares (*grosserie*), and 5 for small articles (*menuierie*), was allowed from 1378. It will be observed that this is of the same quality as the English higher, or Britannia, standard silver, and would be in millièmes ·959 fine.

The remedy was reduced to a uniform one of 2 grains in 1554, and except for this small change, the *argent-le-roy* of 1355 remained the standard until 1797, when the law of 19 Brumaire, Year VI. set up the two present standards in place of it. These are :—

1st standard = ·950, or 11 deniers $9\frac{7}{10}$ grains, fine.
2nd   ,,   = ·800, or 9 deniers $14\frac{1}{8}$ grains, fine.

The remedy allowed is 5 millièmes for either quality.

Modern French silver coin, like the gold coinage, is ·900 fine, or 4·5 silver to ·5 of alloy. This is not so good as the silver of which old French plate was made, nor even as the first quality of modern silver plate, but it is much better than the lower of the two modern standards introduced in 1797.

It must always be remembered that silver francs, like English silver coin, pass current for more than their intrinsic value as metal ; a hectogramme of coinage standard silver being coined in France into 20-franc pieces, whilst its intrinsic value as metal is somewhat less than 16 francs 50 centimes, at the present price of fine silver (say 5 fr. 65 cent. per Troy ounce).

The intrinsic value per hectogramme of French silver of the three modern standards we have had occasion to mention, at present prices and in round numbers may be given as follows :—

$$\left.\begin{array}{l} \cdot950 = 17 \text{ fr. } 25 \text{ cent.} \\ \cdot900 = 16 \text{ fr. } 35 \text{ cent.} \\ \cdot800 = 14 \text{ fr. } 55 \text{ cent.} \end{array}\right\} \text{ per hectogramme.}$$

Fine silver has been taken for the purposes of this calculation to be worth 4s. 6d. per ounce Troy, or about 18 fr. 15 cent. per hectogramme.

CHAPTER II.

THE GOLDSMITHS OF FRANCE, AND THE MARKS USED IN PARIS TILL 1789.

The early goldsmiths of Limoges—St. Martial and St. Eloi—The gold-smiths' guild in Paris—Ancient code for their government—Ordinances of Philippe le Hardi and Philippe le Bel—Letters of confirmation of King John—The craft in the Provinces—The goldsmiths of Montpellier—The Ordinance of 1506—Introduction of date-letters—The Renaissance of Art—List of goldsmiths of the sixteenth century—The school of the Louvre—Destruction of plate under Louis XIV.—Imposition of the droit de marque—The goldsmiths of the seventeenth century—The plate of the Regency—The Rococo period—The classical style—The goldsmiths of the eighteenth century—Summary of the marks on old Paris plate—Table of the Paris date-letters—Table of the marks of the Farmers-General of the duty.

ALTHOUGH the regular records of the Confrèrerie de St. Eloi, as the most ancient of the guilds of goldsmiths in Paris was wont to style itself, do not commence before the middle of the thirteenth century, but little earlier in fact than those of their brethren in London, nowhere do we find such distinct notices of the art of working in the precious metals during the Middle Ages, as in France.

And if France was the nursery of the goldsmith's art in mediæval Europe, Limoges was its cradle. St. Martial, Bishop of Limoges, was known as the patron of the goldsmiths long before the canonization of St. Eloi. It was hard by, at Solignac, that early in the seventh century St. Eloi, who was destined, as it proved, soon to supersede St. Martial in popularity with the craft, founded an abbey, the monks of which, under his skilful direction, devoted themselves to working in gold and silver, and formed a school, whose members went abroad to spread the fame of their founder, and to encourage the art in other cities. Amongst those which profited most by this instruction were Metz, Paris, and Lyons, whose goldsmiths in their turn, and no long time after, rivalled the craftsmen of Limoges itself.

Some few specimens of the work of this period, one at least attributed to St. Eloi's own hand, remain to the present time to attest the skill of these mediæval artists. The Bibliothèque Nationale at Paris can show the chair of Dagobert, whilst the Imperial Treasury of Vienna can boast of the crown and sword of Charlemagne himself.

In the eleventh century French work other than ecclesiastical or royal comes into notice for the first time. John de Garlandia, writing at the end of it, mentions as a separate class of craftsmen the goldsmiths who held *leurs fourneaux et leurs tables sur le Grand Pont*, and made hanaps, buckles, necklaces, pins, and clasps in gold and silver, besides rings set with turquoise, ruby, sapphires, and emeralds. He describes, too, their mode of working as if it were some novelty :—*Le métier de ces orfèvres consiste à battre avec de petits marteaux sur l'enclume, des lames d'or et d'argent et à enchâsser les pierres précieuses dans les chatons des bagues à l'usage des barons et des nobles dames.*

Here, then, we have the first mention of the goldsmiths of Paris already in their famous quarter on the Grand Pont, better known, perhaps, in its connection with their name as the Pont-au-Change, and occupied by them until shaken down once, if not twice, in the course of the thirteenth century, so it is said, by the vibration caused by their hammers.

St. Eloi had by this time quite superseded St. Martial
as their patron, at least in Paris ; his festival day was
kept by the craft with great pomp on the 1st of Decem-
ber in each year, and their processional hymns comme-
morated not only his saintly skill, but even a miracle
wrought by him or for him, a conclusive mark of the
divine favour.

> " Dum vas regi Clothario
> Ex auri massâ fabricat
> Aurum in fabri studio
> Summus Faber multiplicat."

Still there are but few remains of the cunning work of
these ancient guilds. Here and there a *chasse* or reli-
quary of the eleventh or twelfth century is about all
that can be found either in the treasuries of cathedrals
or monasteries, or in the Louvre, Cluny, and other such
collections.

There is better evidence of the frauds of which they
were too often, as it would appear, guilty alike in England and France. Not only are they already open to
the charge of substituting inferior for good gold, but of
gilding and silvering laten and pewter, and selling it for
standard gold or silver, and also of counterfeiting precious stones.

We have incidentally referred, when upon the subject
of English plate, to the well-known code of statutes for
the regulation of the trade guilds of Paris, that was
compiled under these circumstances by direction of
Etienne Boileau, the provost of the city, in 1260.

It is obvious that no trade would require more careful
supervision than that of the goldsmiths, and here it will
be necessary to notice a little more in detail the portion
of the code which relates to this craft, for it is practically
the first definite date we come to in the history of

the Confrèrerie de St. Eloi.   It is a mistake, however,
to consider this event to mark the foundation of the
guild.   In point of fact, the goldsmiths' was only one of
several trades that owed a sort of codification of their
existing traditions to the opportune intervention of the
provost, probably a result of the general move that
seems to have taken place in such matters in the thirteenth century.   Its regulations (which stand eleventh in
the provost's *Livre des Métiers*) seem to have been compiled from the voluntary depositions of the sworn masters
of the craft as to their ancient usages and customs, taken
at the Chatelet, where they were summoned for the
purpose.   It was no new code, though possibly it had
never before been reduced to writing.   Be this as it
may, some of its clauses are of the greatest interest and
importance, and such of them must be given in their
own quaint words :—

> " Il est à Paris orfèvres qui veut et qui faire le set pour qu'il oevre
> ad us et as coustumes du mestier qui tex sunt :
> " Nus orfèvres ne puet ouvrer d'or à Paris qu'il ne soit à la touche
> de Paris ou mieudres laquele touche passe tous les ors de quoi
> on oevre en nule terre.
> " Nus orfèvre ne puet ouvrer à Paris d'argent que il ne soit aussi
> bon comme estelins ou mieudres."

A later clause provides for the good government of the
craft in these terms :—

> " Et est à savoir que li preudome du mestier eslisent ii preudes-
> homes ou iii pour garder le mestier liquel preudhome jurent
> que ils garderont le mestier bien et loiaument as us et as cou-
> stumes devants diz et quand cil preudome ont finé leur service
> li communs du mestier ne les pueent mès remetre à garder le
> mestier devant iii ans se il n'i voleent entrer de leur bone
> volenté."

The other provisions forbid taking more than a single
apprentice unless he be of the family of the master or of
his wife, and forbid taking any apprentice at all for

less than ten years or for less than 100 sols and his keep (*nouriture*) ; they also forbid working at night unless it be for the King, Queen, their children or brothers, or the Bishop of Paris ; they place it upon record that the goldsmith pays no taxes in regard of his craft ; they prescribe the closing of the forges on feast days, with certain exceptions, when the gains are to be devoted to an annual dinner to the poor in the Hôtel Dieu at Paris ; they exempt the craft from " watch " (*guet*), but not from other dues to the King ; and lastly, they enable the ancients to bring any who work bad gold or silver before the provost of Paris, who shall punish them with banishment for four or six years, according to their deserts.

From this time the craft seems to have had a separate existence, with wardens and a common seal ; we should expect, therefore, soon to find it the subject of royal ordinances. And we have no long time to wait, for some fifteen years afterwards, in 1275, Philippe le Hardi obliges all silversmiths working in fine silver to mark their work with the mark (*seign*) of the town they dwell in, under pain of forfeiture, saying nothing, however, at this time about gold. This omission was remedied by a General Ordinance of the month of June, 1313, in which Philippe le Bel enjoins the marking of gold as well as silver, and, more important still, entrusts the care of the town mark (*poinçon*) to two prud'hommes, to be elected in each town for that purpose.

> " Voulons et ordonnons qu'en chaque ville où il y aura orfèvre, ait un seing propre à seigner les ouvrages qui y seront faits et sera gardé par deux prud-hommes establis et esleus à ce faire : et que un seing ne ressemble à l'autre et qui sera trouvé faisant le contraire il perdra l'argent et sera puni de corps et d'avoir."

Here we come to the establishment of the town mark,

or *poinçon de maison commune*. We have already found from the English royal accounts of 1300 that the Paris mark was the *flos glegelli*, or fleur-de-lis, and we know that the standard of gold it denoted was good enough to command its adoption in that year as the authorised English standard for gold wares. It was in 1330 that the Paris goldsmiths could boast of a grant of armorial bearings, the very seal of respectability in that age.

It is highly probable that the craftsmen had even earlier than this been ·in the habit of marking their work each with his own private and peculiar mark ; but there is no positive mention of this custom, if custom it were, as yet.

In Paris, the number of the *gardes*, or wardens, who had charge of the punch, was quickly raised to six, and from 1337 their names are handed down in an unbroken series lasting into the eighteenth century.

Hampered, as they must have been all this time, by the stringent regulations of a sumptuary kind which were prompted by the necessities of Philippe le Bel, and are said by Lacroix not only to have diminished the size of the articles they were allowed to make, but the number and standing of the craftsmen, by not unnatural consequence, the craft, from other accounts, seems to have been in a position to demand, or deserve, in 1355, a renewal of their privileges. The Letters of Confirmation obtained from King John, form the second great landmark in their history, counting the code of Etienne Boileau as the first. They were given at St. Ouen in the month of August, 1355, and contain, amongst others, the following items important for our present purpose.*

---

* *Collection de pièces relatives à l'histoire de France*, par C. Leber, Paris, 1838. Vol. XIX. 348.

" Premièrement. Il est à Paris orfèvre qui veut et qui faire le sect pourtant (pourvu) quil ait ésté aprentis à orfèvre à Paris ou ailleurs aus us et coustumes du mestier ou quil soit tel esprouvé par les maistres et bonnes gens du mestier estre souffisant d'estre orfèvre et de tenir et lever forge et d'avoir poinçon à contreseign.

" 2. Item. Si celuy éprouvé est tel qu'il doive estre orfèvre et avoir poinçon et il a été ouvrier d'autres metaux autres que d'or ne d'argent et il veut etre orfèvre et il le sera mais il n'ouvrera ne fera ouvrer jamais d'autre metal que de bon or et de bon argent, si ce n'est en joyaux d'Eglise commes Tombes, Chasses, Croix, Encensiers ou autre joyaux accoutumez à faire servir Sainte Eglise ou se ce n'est du congié et licence des maistres du mestier et jurra à tenir (forge) et ouvrer aux us et coustumes du mestier qui telles sont.

" 3. Nul orfèvre ne peut ouvrer d'or à Paris qu'il ne soit à la touche de Paris ou meilleur la quelle touche passe tous les ors dont l'on euvre en mille terres, lequel est à dix neuf carats et un quint.

" 12. Nul orfèvre ne peut ouvrer d'argent qui ne se revienne aussi bon comme Argent-le-Roy sans les soudures lequel est dit argent de gros."

Twenty-five other clauses repeat all the regulations collected and recorded in 1260, but in far more minute detail, and provide for the annual election of six wardens, " pour le garde de l'orfèvrerie," with power to reprimand offenders, or at a third offence of bringing them before the provost of Paris.

This charter is noteworthy for several reasons. It illustrates the course of legislation in England, and forms an important point in the history of French marks and standards. In the first place, it definitely mentions a maker's mark for the first time and not only so, but describes it as a punch with a countersign. This countersign has been explained to be some small emblem, such as a heart or other figure of that kind, to be added to the initials of the maker's name for the purpose of distinguishing it more specifically from that of any other maker. In later French this small addition would be called *devise*.

Silver-gilt perfume flask French 17th century.
Victoria & Albert Museum.

It will be observed, too, that the quality of gold of the touch of Paris is defined as gold 19⅕ carats fine. Laborde quotes an entry from the accounts of the Duke of ‚Burgundy of the year 1423, three-quarters of a century later than this, in which "or de touche" is still "xix karas et un quint," and a standard below which one dare not work. It held its own until the middle of the sixteenth century.

Thirdly, the charter brings us to the afterwards familiar "argent le-roy," the quality of which, we may remark in passing, is the same as our English higher, or Britannia, standard silver. It was 11 deniers 12 grains fine, and containing therefore, only one twenty-fourth part of alloy, it must be admitted to have deserved its name.

In 1378, we come upon the first allowance of a remedy or margin from the actual standard, if within which, the metal should be considered as of standard quality.

In that year, Charles V., supplementing the Ordinance of 1355 in this and other respects, at the request of the wardens of the craft, prescribes that the silver used should be "argent qui soit aussi bien et se revienne sans les soudures comme l'argent appelé *l'argent le roi* lequel est a onze deniers douze grains fins, et auront remède de trois grains au marc d'argent et surplus." This remedy is specified to be for large works, and a remedy of five grains and no more is to be allowed for smaller wares. It permits no such tolerance in the case of gold.

All this time the art was flourishing in various provincial towns and cities of France, no less than in Paris ; in fact, the trade must have been in full work everywhere, to judge by the inventories of plate and jewels of the Dukes of Burgundy; of Louis, Duke of Anjou, which was drawn up about the middle of the fourteenth century ; and the other royal and ducal accounts of the same

period. All of these are full of information and interest
for the historian and antiquary.

Letters conveying similar privileges to those already
granted to the goldsmiths of Paris, were, no long time
afterwards, obtained from the same sovereign by their
brethren of Puy-en-Velay (in 1367), and by Troyes (in
1369) ; to which must be added Tours and Bordeaux
about a generation later.   Limoges and Montpellier,
too, maintained their ancient reputation.   Of most of
these cities mention is made in the inventories above
referred to ; and besides Paris, Avignon, Limoges and
Montpellier could boast of styles and standards of their
own, which were well enough known to command special
entry and notice.   Possibly these local standards were
not very high ones : 14 carats, or afterwards 16 carats,
was the gold standard of Puy-en-Velay in this century,
and that of Montpellier seems to have been no higher
than 14.   As early as 1260 there is a warning recorded
against using Montpellier gold ; and its silver was not
first-rate, containing but a third part of alloy, and being
thought good enough if it came out of the fire white.
This quality was actually called "argent de Montpellier."
The curious accounts of the goldsmiths of this city
which have been collected by local archæologists * throw
much light upon our subject generally.   We find from
them that the mode of assay as now practised was in use
in the fourteenth century, and that the workers in gold
and silver there constituted a regular fraternity, governed
by statutes in which the above Montpellier standards
were prescribed, and by which the goldsmiths were
expressly forbidden to manufacture articles in gilt or

---

* Publications de la Société Archéologique de Montpellier, No. 14.
Title *Argentiers.*

silvered copper or brass, save ornaments and utensils for
churches, to mount real stones in jewellery of base metal
or to set false stones in silver or gold.

It appears that by 1355 great abuses had grown up in
the fabrication of articles of silver, and the result of the
consequent disputes between the consuls of the town and
the goldsmiths was that the following regulations for the
trade of goldsmiths were made :—

All vessels and works of silver made by the silversmiths (*argentiers*) of Montpellier were to be of the
standard of 11 deniers and 1 obole, or 12 grains, at the
least. They were to make two patterns, or trial pieces,
of silver of the standard of 11 deniers 14 grains, marked
with the punch of Montpellier, after which they should
work with an allowance or remedy of 2 grains. One
of these trial plates was to be kept at the Consulate, and
the other by the warden of the goldsmiths. A third trial
plate was to be made 11 deniers 1 obole fine, and similarly marked, which was to remain with the consuls for
the trial of suspected works. Every master was to mark
with his own particular mark the pieces of his work, and
to deliver them himself to the warden, who before
marking them with the poinçon of Montpellier was to
remove a portion of the silver, called the *borihl*, which
he was to put into a box, keeping a separate box for each
workman. Once or twice a-year he was to make an
assay of these borihls, and if the standard was found
below the 11 deniers 1 obole, he was to summon the
worker before the consuls, who should make a second
assay, and if they found the fraud confirmed, should
deliver him over to justice. The wardens were to break
such articles as seemed to them insufficient. It is ordered,
moreover, that in assaying the trial pieces and the borihls,
the same ashes, lead and fire should be used ; so it is clear

that the assay was by the cupel.   Nothing had hitherto
been said or done about gold; but though less worked
than silver, there were equal abuses; and in 1401 the
consuls and wardens of the mystery, assisted by several
argentiers, made a regulation in presence of the consuls
of the city by which the standard of gold, which had
been originally only 14 carats, but had by a subsequent
decree been raised to 18 carats, was now reduced to 16,
and there is a question about the trial of gold by the
" touch," showing that it was then in use.

All this may serve to show that the regulations under
which the goldsmiths of Paris worked and the privileges
they obtained, were much the same as those which
ordered and dignified the craft all over France.   Each
city had its mark, and its makers each their *poinçon à
contreseign*.   It may also be inferred from the inventories of the century that the prosperity of the goldsmiths was not, at this time, seriously affected by the
sumptuary laws of which so much is heard both earlier
and later on.   Other troubles indeed they had late in
the century, for the domestic dissensions of the reign of
Charles VI. must have gone far to drive such a craft as
theirs out of the country for security.   Although neither
its work nor the course of its records was actually
broken, there is plenty of evidence that the goldsmiths
of Flanders were largely profiting at the cost of France.
And these troubles ended not with the century.   The
English invasions of the next must have been simply
ruin to the trade.   The goldsmiths of Bruges, Brussels,
Gand, or Dijon, rather than those of France, had name
of note all through the reigns of Charles VII. and
Louis XI., whilst craftsmen of Tours, Blois, Rouen, and
Boulogne are mentioned more often than those of the
capital.   It would be difficult to pick out more than

a dozen names to represent Paris, or even France, for the whole of the fifteenth century, and more difficult still to find any specimens of their work. Herman Roussel was goldsmith to Charles VI., and Hans Croist was of the household of the Duke of Orleans, in the double capacity of goldsmith and " varlet-de-chambre." Gilbert Jehan of Tours is known as the goldsmith of Charles VII.; Jehan Gallant of Charles VIII.; and to these may be added the names of Haliévre, Fernicle, and Barbier, goldsmiths in ordinary to Louis XI. It may be doubted whether these were all Frenchmen. Amongst the provincial craftsmen were André Mangot, Guillaume Poissonier, and Conrad of Cologne, all dwelling at Tours, Michel Blondel at Blois, Jehan Martin at Boulogne; and their names seem of as much consequence in the inventories as if they had been citizens of Paris itself.

Foreign wares of base alloy and without any marks at all were at this time sold, says Lacroix, by itinerant dealers all over the country, and it was not until the very end of the fifteenth century or the beginning of the next, that law and order in these matters began to re-assert themselves.

Signs of reviving prosperity may however be observed about 1470 in the provisions contained in the royal letters to the goldsmiths of Tours in that year, directing that nothing but reliquaries should be made of base metal; and also in the increasing stringency towards the end of the century of the ordinances enjoining on the officers of the Mint the more careful surveillance of the goldsmiths and their work.

In 1506 comes what we may call a third great point in the history of the guild of Paris. By the Ordinance of Blois, given in the month of November in that year, all the goldsmiths were ordered to make themselves new punches, and the sworn masters of the craft were directed to mark all plate with a counter-mark, to be changed every year, registered at the Mint, and stamped upon a copper plate beside the name of the wardens to whom the punch belonged.

Here at last we have distinct mention of what must be the Annual Letter that is always for the future to be found upon Paris plate, at least until 1783.

But, as in England so in France, it is clear that such a letter had been already long in use; and just as the London letter can be traced to 1438, although it is never formally mentioned till 1507, so in Paris an annual letter had certainly been used since 1461.

It is known that a new alphabet began with the letter A on Feb. 5, 1506-7, followed by B on Dec. 10 in the same year 1507, the last-mentioned day being the time of the new wardens' election.

An earlier alphabet, of which the letter M stood for 1472, is referred to by Pierre de Rosnel in the Third Part of his *Mercure Indien*, published in 1667. To this the A of 1506-7 is in proper sequence, 23 letters being always the length of the Paris alphabet; and in the other direction a letter M for 1472 will take us back to 1461 for the commencement of an alphabet half a century older than that of 1506.

It is a curious coincidence, if nothing more, that another cycle of 23 letters would bring us to the year 1431, allowance being made for some irregularity in the election of successive wardens, or within three years of the date at which a date-letter was first used at Montpellier. Each letter, as a rule, represents a set of wardens, whether their period of office endured more or less than a year.

If we turn again to the records of Montpellier we shall see what strong reason there is for crediting that town with the invention of this simple plan of fixing the wardens of each year with their proper responsibilities and of tracing any *laches* to the proper offenders.

In the fifteenth century abuses and frauds in the trade had greatly multiplied. Public clamour was raised against the principal silversmiths for working below the standard of 1355, and a process was instituted against them in 1427. The consuls seized several of their works, had them assayed, found them fraudulent, and made them appear before the tribunal. In their defence they pleaded that the ordinances of 1355 were obsolete with regard to small *orfèvreries*. They were condemned to pay a fine of ten marcs of silver each, and on appeal the sentence was confirmed. Then they claimed exemption from marking girdles and small works ; an inquest was held, and the following ordinances resulted, which were solemnly renewed in 1436 with still stricter conditions. They show with what care the fabrication of works of gold and silver was now regulated. To insure for the future the legal standard, they ordained, besides the ordinary precaution of the box, the borihls, and the mark of the smith, that the name of the warden of the mystery inscribed on the register of the city and on the private book of the silversmith should be followed by one of the letters of the alphabet, which should be reproduced beneath the shield of arms (*écusson*) of the town on each work in order that it might be known under what warden it was marked. The minute detail in which this new plan, and the specific reason for its introduction, are here described, gives the transaction all the appearance of being the original invention of the alphabetical mark, and if so the first invention and adop-

tion of this celebrated and now time-honoured mode of
marking plate must be attributed to the authorities at
Montpellier in 1427. London seems to have followed
suit in 1438, and what more probable than that the
improved security against fraud commended itself to the
goldsmiths of Paris even sooner after its institution at
Montpellier than it reached England, and that they first
adopted the date-letter in 1431.

Whether it will ever be traced to any earlier period or
not, the Paris date-letter appears to have been used with
an almost complete regularity from 1461 ; so much so,
that although some few letters have served for rather
more and others for rather less than a year, if alphabetical tables of twenty-three letters are used (that is to
say, alphabets omitting I or J, U or V, and W), any
letter will fall within a year or so of that in which it was
really used from 1461 to 1783. The slight irregularities
are owing to each letter representing not exactly a year
but the term of office of a particular set of wardens.

We must now go back to 1506 and the ordinance of
Blois, to which is attached the usual clause forbidding
any plate to be made of more than a certain weight, this
time the limit being three marcs in weight and under,
except by authorization of the king. Prohibitions of
this kind were fast becoming insupportable, and indeed
impossible to enforce now that prosperity was reviving
and trade upon the increase. Four years later, in 1510,
all restriction was removed, and the goldsmiths might
fashion articles of any weight they liked, provided only
that they were the proper alloy.

It is at about this time that the goldsmith is said to
have added to his private mark the initial letters of his
Christian name and surname. The maker's mark seems
previously to this to have consisted of some device sur-

mounted by a fleur-de-lis or a crown or both, to which
had been added about the end of the fifteenth century, it
is said in 1493, two small dots or points in allusion to the
two grains of tolerance or remedy which they were allowed.

It must, however, be remarked that the remedy was
three, or, in some cases, five grains from 1378; and that
nothing is positively known of a remedy of two grains
till 1554.

Brighter times are coming with the revival of art,
so well known as the Renaissance, that distinguished
the sixteenth century. For France it was the century
of Francis I. and Henri II., whilst the name of Benvenuto Cellini alone is enough to mark it in the history
of art. The restraints of sumptuary legislation are
heard of no more. The personal interest taken in the
work of the goldsmith by Francis I. was equalled if not
surpassed by that of his successor, and Diana of Poitiers,
the mistress of the latter, is not unjustly called by
Lacroix, the queen of the arts of the Renaissance. It
was under Francis I. that we come upon the first of the
infringements of the rights of the guild by the Crown that
afterwards became more common. However bitterly they
may have resented it, they were not able to prevent the
establishment by this monarch in 1545 of the Hospital of
the Trinity, with certain privileges for such of its inmates
as were goldsmiths. These privileges, although somewhat
abridged from time to time, were still in existence in 1734.

After an abortive and Quixotic attempt in 1540 to
raise the standard of gold-work to absolute purity save
only for a remedy of a quarter of a carat, or at least to
establish a standard of twenty-two carats without any
remedy at all, which was an equally hopeless project,
the very prosperity of the Paris guild, continually on the
increase as it was, almost of itself necessitated its re-

organisation. It had now remained on the same basis
without any reform since 1378. The number as well as
the wealth of the craftsmen had increased with that of
the population generally, and in 1554 the Edict of
Fontainebleau, dated in March of that year, following
close upon and superseding one given at Sainte Menehould a few months earlier, did what the abortive
attempt of 1540 had failed to effect from trying to do
too much. It raised the standard of gold-work for the
future to twenty-two carats with a remedy of a quarter
of a carat ; a similar step to that taken in England by
Queen Elizabeth a very few years later, in 1578. The
French Edict of 1554 did much more than this, limiting
the number of goldsmiths and remedying thereby the
abuses which their excessive numbers had rendered it
impossible to prevent, resettling the always vexed
question of apprenticing, establishing as we have said
a gold standard of twenty-two carats with a remedy of
a quarter of a carat, and a silver standard of 11 deniers
12 grains with a remedy of 2 grains, under heavy
penalties, and regulating the craft in many other par-
ticulars, some of which were modified in the following
year, but not any of those of chief importance. All the
privileges and rights of the guild were solemnly recognized and confirmed by a further set of royal letters
in 1572, granted by Charles IX.

The best known names of the century, besides that
of Cellini, are Pierre Mangot, goldsmith to Francis I.,
Étienne Delaulne, born 1520, and François Dujardin,
goldsmith to Charles IX. in 1574. We must not, however, forget François Briot, who was a goldsmith, though
better known for his masterpieces in pewter, which
were probably models for execution in more precious
metal.

It is impossible to leave this brilliant period without a few more words. Cellini himself testified to the excellent workmanship of the Paris goldsmiths, among whom he found himself on leaving Italy in 1540, and though he worked in Paris but five years before returning to Florence for the rest of his life, his influence was so marked that exception must not be taken to his being reckoned amongst the artists of France for the purposes of this sketch. Few of the works now ascribed to him are so on any authority except their general style and excellence ; but a salt-cellar made for Francis I., which he himself counted for a *chef-d'œuvre*, is preserved at Vienna ; and Lasteyrie specially mentions a magnificent ewer of mounted onyx by his hand which, formerly in the Louvre, is now in the collection of Mr. A. J. Beresford Hope. Of the other names, no doubt that of Etienne Delaulne stands pre-eminent. The interior of his workshop figures on the cover of the South Kensington Museum Penny Handbook on Gold and Silver, as well as in the treatises of Lacroix and Lasteyrie. All these woodcuts are after an engraving preserved in the Bibliothèque Nationale, together with a large number of Delaulne's designs. They are all by the artist's own hand, and are on this account of very great artistic value. Ruling the school of French goldsmiths for nearly a quarter of a century, he seems, especially when working farther east at Strasbourg, to have had no less influence with the craftsmen of Augsburg, and possibly of Nuremberg also. From Augsburg has emanated more than one masterpiece, including the ewers and salvers exhibited by Captain Leyland and Baron James de Rothschild in the Loan Collection at South Kensington in 1862, ornamented with medallions after Delaulne's engraved designs. These bear the Augsburg mark, and are attributed to the last

quarter of the sixteenth century. The goldsmiths of the
end of the century hardly rivalled those of the preceding
generation, though the names of Vimont and of Jean
de la Haye are not unknown.*

The seventeenth century, on entering which we pass
from the fashions of the Renaissance to those of more
modern art, teem with the names of craftsmen of celebrity.
At the very commencement of it we find Henri IV. establishing a royal school of art in the Louvre by letters
patent of 1608, lodging there a number of the most
skilful painters, sculptors, clockmakers, and others, not
forgetting the goldsmiths. Amongst the latter were the
brothers Masbraux, natives of Limoges, after whom
follow in brilliant succession Réné de la Haye, Pierre
Lescot, Alexis Loir, who was one of the first of the
goldsmiths lodged by Louis XIV. at Gobelins, Claude
Ballin, and his equally celebrated son-in-law Nicholas
Delaunay, to whom we must add the name of Pierre
Germain, father of a still more distinguished son.

Where are the works of these favoured artists, so
envied by their brethren for their extraordinary privileges? Alas! it must be said that they are entirely
gone, though some at least, including those of the
famous Ballin, were preserved, or at all events the

---

* CHRONOLOGICAL LIST OF SOME OF THE BEST KNOWN FRENCH
GOLDSMITHS OF THE SIXTEENTH CENTURY.

Matthieu Le Vachet, 1480-1512.

Pierre Mangot, c. 1510-1540;
goldsmith to Louis XII. and
Francis I.

Pirame Triboullet, c. 1529.

Benedict Ramel, c. 1538.

Claude de la Haye, c. 1550; goldsmith to Charles IX.

Etienne Delaulne, b. 1520.

Benvenuto Cellini, 1540-1545.

Claude Marcel, b. 1520.

Richard Routin, temp. Henry II.

Jean Regnard, c. 1570.

Pierre Nicolas, c. 1580.

François Dujardin, c. 1572; goldsmith to Charles IX.

Jean de la Haye, son of Claude;
goldsmith to Gabrielle d'Estrées.

David Vimont, goldsmith to
Henri IV.

memory of them, by the drawings made by Delaunay
before they fell one and all under the ban of 1688.
The destruction of plate in England, under William III.
in 1697, had been anticipated by a far more thorough
holocaust in France, Louis XIV. himself hesitating not
to set the royal example by melting up all that had
rendered the great fête at Versailles in 1668 famous for
all time. It is said that an hundred thousand marcs of
metal, all in masterpieces of Ballin and the other chief
artists of the day, were sacrificed by the Grand Monarque
to State necessities. Much of it consisted of silver tables
and such sumptuous furniture as that of the same date and
fashion which in England is still preserved at Windsor
and Knole to tell of the luxury of the reign of Charles II.
With such an example need it be wondered at that each
loyal noble and courtier followed suit, or that so little
old French plate can now be found, how diligently so-
ever it be searched for by amateur and collector? The
less matters it perhaps that by the Revocation of the
Edict of Nantes in 1685 a number of workmen of great
merit were lost to a country, which would so soon have
sacrificed their choicest productions.

We had almost passed by what is for our purpose one
of the most important steps in our record, namely, the
imposition of a duty on plate by a declaration of 31
March, 1672. Earlier sovereigns had not overlooked
such a means of increasing the revenue ; but attempts in
this direction made by Henri III. and Louis XIII. had
failed, and it was not until the days of Louis XIV. that
the successful imposition of a *droit de marque* incidentally supplies the student with a means for the
future of dating French plate. Hitherto it had borne the
mark of the worker and that of the common hall, which
for some two hundred years had been a date-letter. By

means of this last mark one would suppose that it was a comparatively easy matter to assign a date to any specimen of plate upon which it appears. This is, however, not the case, or at all events it is a much greater difficulty than in the case of English plate, owing first to the smaller difference that there is between the style of one French alphabet and another, and secondly to there being, in the case of French plate, no such additional marks as the lion passant and leopard's head crowned, which are so great a help for dating old English plate. In point of fact it is not until 1672 that the addition of the mark of the farmer of the duty, enables us to identify with certainty the year signified by any particular alphabetical letter.

The mark of the farmer was to be the Mint letter of the town surmounted by a fleur-de-lis, and a new design for the letter was adopted by each successive tenant of that perhaps lucrative post. From 1672 French plate bears this third mark, called the *poinçon de charge*, in addition to the other two. For Paris it was the letter A.

A fourth but less important mark was added in 1681, when the farmers obtained the right of marking plate both in its rough state and again when finished; the one mark by way of denoting its liability to the charge, and the second certifying to its due payment or discharge. This fourth mark was called the *poinçon de décharge*.

From 1681 there are accordingly four Paris marks; and the punches of the charge and discharge used by each successive farmer of the duty being of different fashion from those of any of his predecessors in office, enable us to fix the date of any alphabetical letter with which they are found, the names, dates, and marks of each farmer being known. Thus it will be observed by the aid of the tables at the end of this chapter that the letter S of 1734 can be as readily distinguished from that of 1711 as from those for 1758 or 1781 ; the letter for 1734 being associated with the punch of the farmer-general, Hubert Louvet, and the other letters with one or other of the quite different punches affected by his predecessor, Etienne Baligny, or his successors in administration, Eloi Brichard and Henri Clavel. The publication of these marks will, for the first time as the author believes, enable the English amateur to fix the date of specimens of old French plate, at least from 1672 ; and there is very little older plate left for him to date, owing to the circumstances we have narrated. These punches remained in use until the abolition of all taxes in 1791.

The size of the maker's mark as well as of the date-letter was fixed in 1679 as two lines high by one and a quarter wide, a matter which had hitherto been left to individual discretion.

It is amid the lamentations of writers on French art that we have arrived at the end of the seventeenth century—lamentations on the decay of taste which relegated the task of designing to a school of architects and sculptors who had but one style for everything. " *On ne mettait pas de différence,*" says Lacroix, " *entre la décoration monumentale d'un hôtel et celle d'une église ; on ne croyait pas qu'une statue de saint ou d'apôtre devait peu ressembler à celle d'un demi-dieu païen, on manquait de ce sentiment qui fait l'art s'inspire toujours de son but et de son objet.*" It may be admitted that the plate of the days of Louis XIV. was far too gross and massive in style to be actually pleasing, but some there are who choose

" Old plate,
Not for its beauty, but its weight ;

and many good judges have a real admiration, if only
half avowed, for the work of the school that was ruled
over by Mansard and Lebrun.   It has merits of its own,
even if it does not appeal to every standard of taste ;
it is characteristic of its time, and worse styles have had
their day.*

Between this and what may be called the *Rococo*
period, there comes the same transitional style in French,
that is noticed in the history of English, art.   We have
in England the plain, perhaps too plain, plate of William
and Queen Anne, of which gadrooning was almost the
only ornament, yielding to the sort of decoration that
we associate with the name of Hogarth before it is
covered with the exquisite chasing, chiefly in flowers,
insects, and other natural objects, of the later days of
Paul Lamerie.   In France we find the style that has
been aptly called the style of the Regency, prevailing
from about 1710 to 1735, and leading up by a natural
step to the period of Louis XV.

For a time the dire necessity which compelled the
sacrifice of every art treasure of intrinsic value in 1688
served also to forbid or delay their being replaced ; and
with such rigour were the ordinances in that behalf
enforced, that the trade of the goldsmith may be almost

---

* CHRONOLOGICAL LIST OF SOME OF THE BEST KNOWN FRENCH
GOLDSMITHS OF THE SEVENTEENTH CENTURY.

Réné de la Haye, 1620–1640 ; gold-
  smith to Mazarin.
Pijard, *c.* 1630.
Pierre Lescot.
Jacques Delaunay.
Pierre Baille, *c.* 1646.
Mellin, 1650–1700.
Claude Ballin, *b.* 1615, *d.* 1678 ;
  goldsmith to Louis XIV.

Alexis Loir, *b.* 1640, *d.* 1713.
Nicholas Delaunay,   1678–1727;
  son-in-law of Ballin.
Pierre Germain, died young
  1682.
Pierre Bain, *c.* 1685.
Montarsy, *c.* 1690.
Louis Loir, 1692–1710.

The Burghley Nef, a nautilus shell mounted in silver parcel-gilt. Mark of Pierre Le Flamand and the Paris mark of 1482. Height 34.6 cm. Victoria & Albert Museum.

said to have been in a state of suspended animation until about 1720. The age of copper, says Lacroix, had succeeded to the age of gold and the age of silver.

Nevertheless, some means were found of educating the skilful hands of the younger Ballin, of Thomas Germain, so celebrated for his toilet services, and of a Besnier, names which no long time afterwards compose a group, the mere mention of whose work is enough to send the French connoisseur of their style into a rhapsody.* And, truth to say, this high esteem is not unjustified, for to the eye wearied with the ostentatious grandeur and weight of an earlier school, the fine chasing which now came into fashion, and exquisitely graduated bas-reliefs, with their pleasing effects of light and shade, had an irresistible charm. Curiously enough, the texture of the metal used at this time sometimes strikes one as rather coarse-grained, and even when highly ornamented and chased looks rather like what iron-founders call " fine cast." This is probably due to the alloying metal.

It is to the goldsmiths of Paris that nearly all the finest examples of this period are to be ascribed. In France, as was also the case in England, the capital was

---

* It has been thus happily described by a distinguished French amateur:—" Dans ce style aimable et tout français, si français qu'il n'a guère été imité à l'étranger, on trouve la correction et la grandiose du style de Louis XIV., mais dépouillé de sa raideur. La grâce la plus parfaite, l'esprit le plus ingénieux, le goût le plus riant, viennent se joindre à l'ampleur, à la noblesse, à la solidité des ouvrages du grand siècle. Dans l'orfèvrerie, les artistes travaillant dans ce style ont fort usé du chanlevé, c'est-à-dire, de ces ornements pris sur pièce avec un relief très-doux, mais assez fort pour préparer la voie à ces effets de lumière, qui donnent tant de valeur et de charme à l'ornementation des métaux ; cela ne les a pas empêchés d'user du haut-relief, avec une douceur et un fini de ciselure qu'on ne saurait trop louer."

now able to attract and keep the best talent of the craft
in its permanent service ; and this is not so much the
effect of royal patronage or the influence of the schools
of the Louvre and Gobelins, as of a centralisation that
has never since relaxed its force.

Sumptuary legislation at last entirely gave way before
modern enlightenment and the growing luxury of the
times, and the year 1721 makes an end of restrictions,
at all events as to the use of silver, which would in any
case have been out of joint with the days of Madame de
Pompadour and the Dubarry.

At the same time a second standard of twenty and a
quarter carats, with a remedy of a quarter of a carat,
was allowed for gold wares of small size.

Unfettered, then, by antiquated legislation, and fos-
tered by the great ladies of the Court of Louis XV., the
full tide of the *Rococo* period succeeds to the fashions of
the Regency. Nicholas Besnier gives place to his son-
in-law Roettiers, and the chaste style of Germain to the
caprices of the *goût de rocailles* which were affected even
by Ballin.

As in the last generation, so now in 1759, much good
work was melted up almost as soon as made, the King
again leading in the patriotic sacrifice, followed by the
princes of the blood, the Dauphinesse, Madame de Pompadour, Belleisle, and Choiseul.

From this to the Revolution of 1789, there is only
a single step, but before taking it, passing mention must
be made of a name that has made itself famous in the
annals of the goldsmiths of Paris. It was to Pierre
Le Roy, one of their past wardens, that they owed a
complete code of their statutes and privileges of their
guild, as they were in 1734. It is only less valuable
than the old compilation of Etienne Boileau ; and it is

the more to be lamented that the scope of his researches
did not include the ancient marks used by the corpora-
tion as well as its ancient privileges, for it is clear that
he had access to sources of information that have now
for ever disappeared. Though it is not a chronological
account verified by references, it is nevertheless a complete summary of all that then regulated the craft,
arranged in chapters and clauses for the use and guidance
of the wardens and craftsmen of the day. For us it
may serve to show what of the various regulations we
have noticed remained in force in his time.

We gather from it that the government of the guild
remained the same as we have given it ; that the standards both of gold and silver were unaltered—notice
being taken of the then new one of a second quality of
gold, introduced under Louis XV. only a few years
before ;—and that the counter-mark, or *poinçon de
Paris*, was in the same careful keeping as ever.

The number of Paris goldsmiths was still three hundred, as fixed in 1612 ; but those who dwelt within the
privileges of the Hospital of the Trinity, as well as those
of the Louvre and Gobelins, and also those who enjoyed
arrêts and letters patent, were considered supernumerary
to this established limit. All alike were recognised as
members of the guild for every other purpose.

The goldsmith's own mark was to be a punch bearing
a fleur-de-lis crowned, with his name and device ; its
size was to be as before, two lines high by one and a
quarter wide.

They were to keep in their shops tables of the value
of the marc of gold and silver, of the prescribed standards according to which they ought to work, and of
the sub-divisions of the marc weight.

There are a few other clauses of interest, amongst

them one that shows how carefully the ability and
knowledge of aspirants for the honourable position of
mastership in the craft was inquired into by the wardens.
They were charged to examine such aspirants not only
in the sub-divisions of the marc weight and the prices
and alloys of gold and silver wares, but in the manner
of alloying base and fine metal so as to render it of the
quality required by the various ordinances. The wardens were also to inform themselves as to the manners
and moral conduct of such candidates.

Another good regulation is that which requires the
goldsmith to sell the metal of their works separately, as
it were, from the fashion, distinguishing in the bills
rendered to customers the amount paid for material and
for workmanship respectively.

It may here be remarked in passing, that from 1749
foreign plate imported into France was to be marked
with a punch representing the letters ET, or else the
single letter E.

Let us now take the last step in our historical sketch.
To complete it, there remains but the reign of Louis XVI.
and its well-known classical style, which found an exact
counterpart in English art. The same oval pointed
vases, the same hanging wreaths of flowers or folds of
drapery, tied up with knots of riband and carried over
medallions, which are found in England first in the days
of the two brothers Adam, and are perpetuated in the
designs of Flaxman, form the principal features in
French art also ; and if there is anything to distinguish the goldsmiths of Paris from those of London,
it must be the skill which the former lavished upon small
objects, such as snuff-boxes, bonbonnières, étuis, and the
like.

Two members of the family of Ducrollay, P. J.

Antoine, J. George, C. B. Sageret, and A. J. M. Vachette, are amongst the best known of this school, which Lasteyrie, in his *Histoire de l'Orfèvrerie*, considers to have been the single branch of the goldsmith's art which really flourished in the last quarter of the eighteenth century. R. J. Auguste was almost the only great goldsmith of the reign of Louis XVI.*

---

* CHRONOLOGICAL LIST OF SOME OF THE BEST KNOWN FRENCH GOLD-SMITHS OF THE EIGHTEENTH CENTURY. THE DATES ARE TAKEN CHIEFLY FROM THOSE ASSIGNED BY THE BARON J. PICHON TO VARIOUS ARTICLES IN THE CATALOGUE OF THE LENOIR GIFT TO THE MUSEUM OF THE LOUVRE; AND FROM THE PUBLISHED CATALOGUE OF THE ANCIENT PLATE IN HIS OWN CELEBRATED COLLECTION.

J. B. Loir, 1701.

Claude Ballin, nephew of Claude the Elder, 1700–1750.

Jacques Ballin, nephew of Claude, 1719–1750; goldsmith to Louis XV.

Ch. François Croze, 1725.

Paul Soulaine, 1726.

Nicholas Besnier, 1728–1737; goldsmith to Louis XV.

Remy Chatria, 1728.

Syrieys, 1729.

Antoine Plot, 1733.

Nicholas Outrebon, 1733.

Louis Renard, 1733.

Thomas Germain, 1726–1747; *b.* 1675, son of Pierre.

J. Ducrollay, 1734–1761.

J. A. Meissonnier, 1735.

J. C. Ducrollay, 1737–1761.

P. J. Antoine, 1739–1743.

Charles Roettiers, *c.* 1745; son-in-law of N. Besnier.

Ed. Pierre Balzac, 1744.

Simon Bourguet, 1744–1750.

J. Moynat, 1745–1761.

Antoine Jean de Villeclair, 1750–1764.

J. George, 1752–1762.

Ch. B. Sageret, 1752–1764; goldsmith to the Duke of Orléans.

P. J. Bellangé, 1754–1762.

Mathieu Coiny, 1755–1772.

L. F. A. Taunay, 1761–1773.

François Joubert, 1765–1785.

François Thomas Germain, 1764; son of Thomas.

J. E. Blerzy, 1768–1781.

J. F. Mathis de Beaulieu, 1768–1777.

Robert Joseph Antoine, 1770.

J. B. Roettiers, 1770.

Denis Franckson, 1770–1780.

Pierre Jean Lenfant, 1772–1776.

B. Pillieu, 1774–1779.

C. N. Delanoy, 1775.

J. C. Vauconverberghen, 1775.

Ant. Boullier, 1775.

Ch. Spriman, 1776–1778.

J. B. Chéret, 1766–1785.

Louis J. M. Bouty, 1778.

A. J. M. Vachette, 1779–1806.

J. L. D. Outrebon, 1773–1782.

J. N. Saget, 1783–1789.

R. L. Dany, 1786.

If nothing else survived, we may the less regret the general shipwreck of 1789, in which the history of old French plate and its marks comes to a sudden and disastrous end. The time-honoured series of Parisian date-letters had already terminated in 1783, the first of many coming changes. For the six remaining years up to 1789, the *poinçon de maison commune* was the letter P crowned, and the stamp was to bear, in the hollow between the crown and the letter, the last two figures of the date (*e.g.*, 84 for 1784), or else some small secret and variable device.* Some think that the mark used in 1789 will be found on plate up to 1791, and perhaps till 19 Brumaire, Year VI. (1797). But the famous statute of this last year, being the foundation of the modern system of hall-marking, must be considered in a later chapter.

SUMMARY.

To sum up ; the marks that will be found on plate made in Paris before 1791 are as follows :—

1. The punch of the common hall (*poinçon de maison commune*) from 1275-1791.
2. The maker's mark (*poinçon du maître*) from very early times.
3. The mark of the farmer of the duties (*poinçon de charge*) from 1672–1791.
4. A second duty mark (*poinçon de décharge*) from 1681–1791.

Of each of these marks a few words in turn, after devoting a few lines to each of the sets of Paris marks given opposite for the sake of illustrating the following summary and tables. The special points in which they

---

* It certainly bore such small numerals in some of these years; the fashion of the letter P varying each twelvemonth.

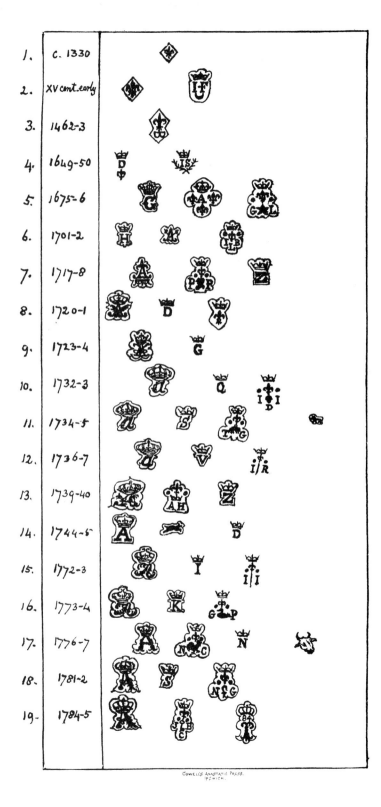

1.	c. 1330
2.	XV cent. early
3.	1462-3
4.	1649-50
5.	1675-6
6.	1701-2
7.	1717-8
8.	1720-1
9.	1723-4
10.	1732-3
11.	1734-5
12.	1736-7
13.	1739-40
14.	1744-5
15.	1772-3
16.	1773-4
17.	1776-7
18.	1781-2
19.	1784-5

serve to illustrate the history of hall-marking are pointed out in each case :—

1. A bowl or deep plate with a pattern of beaten work, found with a coin of 1330 and other things at Rouen. No. 109. 65. South Kensington Museum.

  This shows the touch of Paris in a lozenge, as it often appears in the fourteenth and the early part of the following century. At the beginning of the fourteenth the sign of the town was the only mark prescribed.

2. A chalice of the first half of the fifteenth century, belonging to the domestic chapel at Rhûg in Wales. Noted by W. W. E. Wynne, Esq.

  This shows a maker's mark with initials and a crescent for device, in addition to the touch of Paris, which last is still in a lozenge.

3. A beaker or cup diapered with chains of SS, having crowned Lombardic 𝕰 𝕰's between them. Oriel College, Oxford.

  This, which is called the Founder's Cup, is more properly attributed by Mr. Shaw and others to Prince Edward, son of King Henry VI., its style and the engraved letters all pointing to the same conclusion. It will be remembered that his mother, Queen Margaret, was in France in 1462 seeking the aid of the French king after the disastrous battle of Towton, her husband and young son having fled into Scotland. The hall mark gives the touch of Paris, still in a lozenge, combined with the year letter for 1462-3.

4. A chalice, dated 1650. Abbey of St. Maurice, Canton Valais.

  This gives a maker's mark, and the year letter used in Paris for 1649-50, crowned as it is found for the future, but still accompanied by the lily of the touch of Paris, which was soon afterwards discontinued. The maker's mark gives initials and crossed branches for a device.

5. A standing crucifix, about 27 in. high. Messrs. Lamberts.

  Here we have an early example of the mark of the charge, it being that used by the very first farmer general (Fortier, 1672-80); in the maker's mark will be observed the device of a mullet, and the two pellets. Date-letter for 1675-6.

6. A two-handled flower-vase ornamented with gadroons, &c. Baron J. Pichon.

  This shows the mark of the charge (Perrine, 1698–1703), the date-letter for 1701-2 and the mark attributed by Baron J. Pichon to J. B. Loir, a member of a family of hereditary goldsmiths.

7. A tumbler or round-bottomed drinking cup. The author.

> Shows the mark of the charge (Sollier, 1713–17), the year letter for 1716–7, and a maker's mark with a helmet for device between the initials P. P.

8. A pair of salt-cellars. Noted by Octavius Morgan, Esq.

> These show the mark of the charge and also of the discharge (Et. de Bouges, 1717–21), and the year letter for 1720–1.

9. Pair of octagonal silver boxes, exhibited by Lord Bateman. No. 6413, South Kensington Loan Cat. 1862.

> The mark of the charge (Cordier, 1722–27); year letter for 1723–4.

10. A tea-pot, fluted and chased with festoons of finely cut foliage. 4271. 57. South Kensington Museum.

> Charge mark (H. Louvet, 1732–38); year mark for 1732–3; maker's mark with acorn for device.

11. A pair of table candlesticks in the style of the Regency. W. A. T. Amherst, Esq., M.P.

> These bear the same mark of the charge as the last, with the year letter for 1734–5. The maker's mark, T G with a fleece, is that of the celebrated Thomas Germain. It may be remarked that his mark is so rarely to be found in France, that the Baron J. Pichon has only been able to note three examples in Paris collections.

12. Small salt-cellars. Berkeley Castle.

> These give the same mark of the charge, with the year letter for 1736–7.

13. A tall gadrooned chalice on baluster stem. Messrs. Taburet, Paris.

> The charge mark (Robin, 1738–44); year mark for 1739–40.

14. Wine-tasting bowl or cup, with a medal of Louis XV. inserted in the bottom. Octavius Morgan, Esq.

> Mark of the charge and discharge (L'Echaudel, 1744–50), with the year letter for 1744–5.

15. Soup-tureen with scroll feet and fruit for handle, engraved with Beauharnais arms. Sold at Christie and Manson's in 1875.

> Charge mark (Alaterre, 1768–74), with the year letter for 1772–3.

16. Engraved beaker or tumbler on foot. Mr. W. Boore.

> Charge mark as before, year mark for 1773–4, maker's mark with a duck for device between the initials.

17. Shows the discharge mark of a bull's head in addition to the charge (J. B. Fouache, 1774–80); maker's mark with a cock for device.

18. Gives charge mark (Clavel, 1780–9); letter for 1781–2; maker's initials with a crozier head for device.

19. Pair of circular toilet boxes, engraved with the arms of De
 Rohan. A. W. Franks, Esq.

> These give the same charge mark as the last, but with
> the crowned P and 84, which was the Paris mark for
> 1784. The maker's mark is that of J. B. Cheret,
> being his initials with a key. These boxes have never
> been sold, but have passed always by gift or bequest,
> through various hands, from the Duchess de Rohan
> to the late Mr. Felix Slade, and from him to their
> present owner.

We now return to our summary of what has been said
as to each mark, beginning with

THE PUNCH OF THE COMMON HALL.

This was first appointed by Philippe le Hardi in 1275,
and was in early times the fleur-de-lis (flos glegelli).
There is reason to think that in the fifteenth century
it was borne upon a lozenge, or diamond, shaped
stamp.

An ancient chalice of French make and of the fifteenth
century bears the mark thus.

Afterwards, say from 1461–1783, it was a letter of
the alphabet crowned. This was probably at first a
letter added to the fleur-de-lis rather than substituted
for it.

The beaker at Oriel College, Oxford, seems to be of
Paris make in 1462, and it bears the fleur-de-lis on a
diamond, the lower part of which is cut off and enlarged
into a second but smaller diamond-shaped space, containing the Roman capital letter B placed thus ⬚ across
the bottom of the fleur-de-lis.

A letter D, apparently standing for 1649-50, has a
crown above and a fleur-de-lis beneath the letter.

After this, and from about the middle of the seventeenth

century the letter seems to have been simply crowned,
and so remained till 1783-4.*

From 1784 the letter P crowned was substituted for
the alphabetical letter as the Paris mark, the punch at
first bearing the last two figures of the date (*e. g.* 84 for
1784) between the crown and the letter, the shape of
which varied each year.

This new system of marking only lasted till 1789,
though some think that the mark for 1789 did duty till
1791, if not until 1797.

THE MAKER'S MARK.

This was no doubt used long before it is actually mentioned or prescribed by any statute.

In the fourteenth century it was a punch with a
counter-sign, which consisted of some small emblem or
device, with a fleur-de-lis or a crown or both.

To this was afterwards added, it is said in 1493, the
two small points or dots which are commonly observed
in the marks of French goldsmiths.

By 1506 the maker had added the initials of his name ;
some had perhaps used their initials as part of their
mark long before. In 1679 the size of the maker's mark
was fixed by statute at two lines high by one line and a
quarter wide.

The goldsmiths who followed the Court, and those who
were lodged at Gobelins, early in the eighteenth century,
do not seem to have marked their work. Baron J.
Pichon notes that the wares of those who belonged to

---

* The alphabets appear to consist
almost entirely of Roman capital
letters, some of them enclosed in a
plain escutcheon, others merely
countersunk on a punch of the
shape of the letter.

*Silver porringer with the mark of N. Outreban
and the Paris mark of 1759. Height 12.6 cm.
Victoria & Albert Museum.*

the Hospital of the Trinity have a triangle in the maker's mark to distinguish them.

THE MARKS OF THE FARMER OF THE DUTY.

The first mark adopted on the imposition of a plate duty in 1672 was the Mint-letter of the Town under a fleur-de-lis. This was called the *poinçon de charge*, and for Paris it was the letter A.

In 1681 the farmers obtained permission to have plate stamped when finished as well as in the rough, by way of better security for the collection of the tax. The second mark, invented for that purpose, and called the *poinçon de décharge*, was a small one, usually a human head or that of some beast or bird. The first mark would now admit the liability of the article receiving it to pay duty, and the second would acknowledge its due payment. These two marks lasted till the abolition of all taxes in 1791, and a list of them in their successive variations is given next after the tables of Paris date-letters appended to this chapter.

It should be remarked that from 1768 there was a special *poinçon de décharge* for objects that were marked *gratis*. This was a royal crown, and it would be applied, instead of any other mark *de décharge*, on articles made for such personages, royal or official, as might be exempt from liability to the duty.

TABLES OF THE ALPHABETICAL DATE-LETTERS USED IN PARIS FROM
1461-2—1783-4.

	LOUIS XI.		
A	1461-2	1484-5	1506-7 (Feb. 5, 1506 -7—Dec., 1507)
B	1462-3	1485-6	1507-8 (from Dec. 10, 1507)
C	1463-4	1486-7	1508-9
D	1464-5	1487-8	1509-10
E	1465-6	1488-9	1510-1
F	1466-7	1489-90	1511-2
G	1467-8	1490-1	1512-3
H	1468-9	1491-2	1513-4
I	1469-70	1492-3	1514-5
			FRANCIS I.
K	1470-1	1493-4	1515-6
L	1471-2	1494-5	1516-7
M	1472-3	1495-6	1517-8
N	1473-4	1496-7	1518-9
O	1474-5	1497-8	1519-20
		LOUIS XII.	
P	1475-6	1498-9	1520-1
Q	1476-7	1499-1500	1521-2
R	1477-8	1500-1	1522-3
S	1478-9	1501-2	1523-4
T	1479-80	1502-3	1524-5
U	1480-1	1503-4	1525-6
X	1481-2	1504-5	1526-7
Y	1482-3	1505-6	1527-8
	CHARLES VIII.		
Z	1483-4	1506-7 (to Feb. 5, 1506-7)	1528-9

TABLES OF THE ALPHABETICAL DATE-LETTERS USED IN PARIS FROM
1461-2—1783-4—*continued.*

A	1529–30	1552–3	1575–6
B	1530–1	1553–4	1576–7
C	1531–2	1554–5	1577–8
D	1532–3	1555–6	1578–9
E	1533–4	1556–7	1579–80
F	1534–5	1557–8	1580–1
G	1535–6	1558–9	1581–2
		FRANCIS II.	
H	1536–7	1559–60	1582–3
		CHARLES IX.	
I	1537–8	1560–1	1583–4
K	1538–9	1561–2	1584–5
L	1539–40	1562–3	1585–6
M	1540–1	1563–4	1586–7
N	1541–2	1564–5	1587–8
O	1542–3	1565–6	1588–9
			HENRY IV.
P	1543–4	1566–7	1589–90
Q	1544–5	1567–8	1590–1
R	1545–6	1568–9	1591–2
S	1546–7	1569–70	1592–3
	HENRY II.		
T	1547–8	1570–1	1593–4
U	1548–9	1571–2	1594–5
X	1549–50	1572–3	1595–6
Y	1550–1	1573–4	1596–7
		HENRY III.	
Z	1551–2	1574–5	1597–8

TABLES OF THE ALPHABETICAL DATE-LETTERS USED IN PARIS FROM
1461-2—1783-4—*continued.*

A	1598-9	1621-2	1645-6
B	1599-1600	1622-3	1646-7 and 47-8
C	1600-1	1623-4	1648-9
D	1601-2	1624-5	1649-50
E	1602-3	1625-6	1650-1
F	1603-4	1626-7	1651-2
G	1604-5	1627-8	1652-3
H	1605-6	1628-9	1653-4
I	1606-7	1629-30	1654-5
K	1607-8	1630-1	1655-6
L	1608-9	1631-2	1656-7
M	1609-10	1632-3 and 33-4	1657-8
N	LOUIS XIII. 1610-1	1634-5	1658-9
O	1611-2	1635-6	1659-60 (Dec. 11, 1659—July 1, 1660)
P	1612-3	1636-7	1660-1 (from July 1, 1660)
Q	1613-4	1637-8	1661-2
R	1614-5	1638-9	1662-3
S	1615-6	1639-40	1663-4
T	1616-7	1640-1	1664-5
U	1617-8	1641-2	1665-6
X	1618-9	1642-3	1666-7
Y	1619-20	LOUIS XIV. 1643-4	1667-8
Z	1620-1	1644-5	1668-9

TABLES OF THE ALPHABETICAL DATE-LETTERS USED IN PARIS FROM
1461-2—1783-4—*continued.*

A	1669-70	1694-5	1717-8
B	1670-1	1695-6	1718-9
C	1671-2	1696-7	1719-20
D	1672-3	1697-8	1720-1
E	1673-4	1698-9	1721-2
F	1674-5	1699-1700	1722-3
G	1675-6	1700-1	1723-4
H	1676-7	1701-2	1724-5
I	1677-8	1702-3	1725-6
K	1678-9 and 79 (July 1678—Jan. 1, 1679-80	1703-4	1726-7
L	1680-1 (Jan. 1, 1679-80—July, 1681)	1704-5	1727-8
M	1681-2 (from July 1681)	1705-6	1728-9
N	1682-3	1706-7	1729-30
O	1683-4	1707-8	1730-1
P	1684-5	1708-9	1731-2
Q	1685-6	1709-10	1732-3
R	1686-7	1710-1	1733-4
S	1687-8	1711-2	1734-5
T	1688-9	1712-3	1735-6
U or V	1689-90	1713-4	1736-7
X	1690-1 and 1691-2 (July 20, 1690 — Oct. 13, 1692)	1714-5	1737-8
		LOUIS XV.	
Y	1692-3 (from Oct. 13, 1692)	1715-6	1738-9
Z	1693-4	1716-7	1739-40

TABLES OF THE ALPHABETICAL DATE-LETTERS USED IN PARIS FROM
1461-2—1783-4—*continued.*

A	1740–1 and 41–2 (Dec. 29, 1740— Mar. 9, 1742)	1764–5
B	1742–3 (from Mar. 9, 1742–3—July, 1743)	1765–6
C	1743–4 (from July, 1743)	1766–7
D	1744–5	1767–8
E	1745–6	1768–9
F	1746–7	1769–70
G	1747–8	1770–1
H	1748–9	1771–2
I	1749–50	1772–3
K	1750–1	1773–4
		LOUIS XVI.
L	1751–2	1774–5
M	1752–3	1775–6
N	1753–4	1776–7
O	1754–5	1777–8
P	1755–6	1778–9
Q	1756–7	1779-80
R	1757–8	1780–1
S	1758–9	1781–2
T	1759–60	1782–3
U or V	1760–1	1783–4 (from July 12, 1783)
X	1761–2	
Y	1762–3	
Z	1763–4	

LIST OF THE FARMERS GENERAL OF THE DUTIES AND THEIR
MARKS FROM 1672.

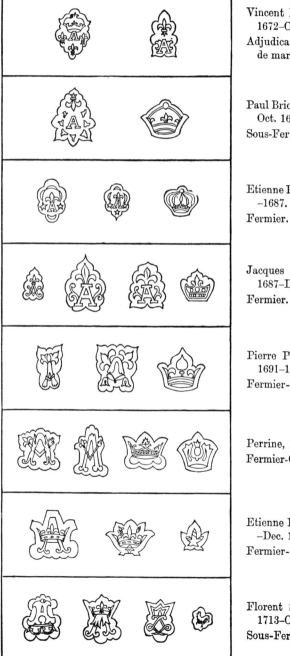

Vincent Fortier, Oct.
  1672–Oct. 1680.
Adjudicataire du droit
  de marque.

Paul Brion de Saussoy,
  Oct. 1680–1684.
Sous-Fermier.

Etienne Ridereau, 1684
  –1687.
Fermier.

Jacques Leger, Oct.
  1687–Dec. 1691.
Fermier.

Pierre Pointeau, Dec.
  1691–1698.
Fermier-Général.

Perrine, 1698–1703.
Fermier-Général.

Etienne Baligny, 1703
  –Dec. 1713.
Fermier-Général.

Florent Sollier, Dec.
  1713–Oct. 1717.
Sous-Fermier.

LIST OF THE FARMERS GENERAL, ETC.—*continued.*

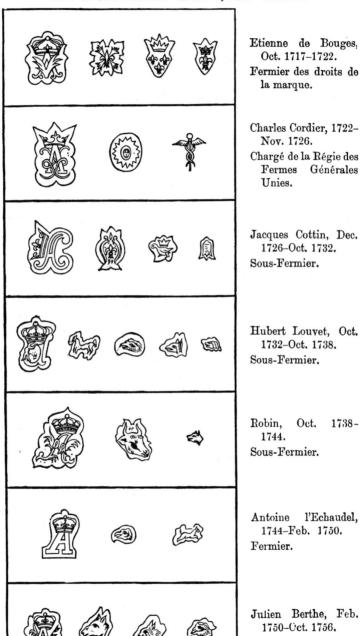

Etienne de Bouges, Oct. 1717–1722.
Fermier des droits de la marque.

Charles Cordier, 1722–Nov. 1726.
Chargé de la Régie des Fermes Générales Unies.

Jacques Cottin, Dec. 1726–Oct. 1732.
Sous-Fermier.

Hubert Louvet, Oct. 1732–Oct. 1738.
Sous-Fermier.

Robin, Oct. 1738–1744.
Sous-Fermier.

Antoine l'Echaudel, 1744–Feb. 1750.
Fermier.

Julien Berthe, Feb. 1750–Oct. 1756.
Sous-Fermier.

LIST OF THE FARMERS GENERAL, ETC.—*continued.*

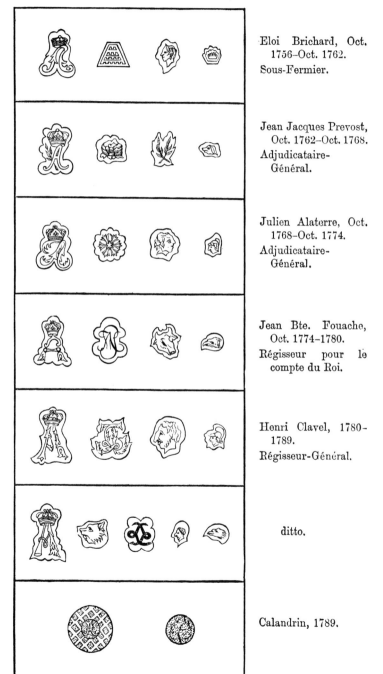

Eloi Brichard, Oct. 1756–Oct. 1762. Sous-Fermier.

Jean Jacques Prevost, Oct. 1762–Oct. 1768. Adjudicataire-Général.

Julien Alaterre, Oct. 1768–Oct. 1774. Adjudicataire-Général.

Jean Bte. Fouache, Oct. 1774–1780. Régisseur pour le compte du Roi.

Henri Clavel, 1780–1789. Régisseur-Général.

ditto.

Calandrin, 1789.

CHAPTER III.

PROVINCIAL MARKS TILL 1789.

Ancient provincial hall-marks—The Mint letters of provincial centres—
The marks of 1783—The standards of Burgundy and Lorraine—
Table of arms of towns where plate was made before 1783—Table of
the marks used under the administration of Jn. Bte. Fouache, 1774-
1780—Table comparing Paris and Provincial marks—Table of the
town marks used from 1783-1789.

MOST of the ordinances that have been already considered apply to the goldsmiths of the provinces as well
as those of Paris. Some of the provincial communities
were, as we have seen, of ancient foundation. If Marseilles and Bordeaux alone can trace the history of their
goldsmiths' guilds to the thirteenth century, Cambrai,
Puy-en-Velay, Rouen, and Troyes can go back as far as
the fourteenth, whilst Toulouse and Montpellier both
obtained royal recognition in the fifteenth century.

Goldsmiths must have worked in many of these places
even earlier, for Philippe le Hardi in 1275 directs the
goldsmiths everywhere to mark their work with the
seign of the town in which they dwell.

This mark appears in very many cases to have been
a shield of the town arms. Montpellier early in the
fifteenth century, when adopting a date-letter, appoints
that it shall be " reproduced beneath the shield of arms
of the town " on the work. The most ancient specimens
known of the work of Strasbourg craftsmen bear for
town mark a shield with a bend, which is the armorial

bearing of that city ; whilst a very ancient spoon with an acorn head, found at Rouen, but now in the South Kensington Museum, bears in the bowl a lamb and flag. In some places, however, they seems to have used, at least in early times, the first two letters of the name of the town, or the first letters of each syllable of it, or sometimes its first and last letters.

The author is inclined to attribute the mark consisting of the letters $\overline{\text{M}}\text{O}\overset{.}{\text{P}}$ in Lombardic characters, which occurs on a basin or deep plate of the fourteenth century in the South Kensington Museum, to Montpellier. **AM** in the same style of lettering seems at one time to have been used at Amiens. Whether the arms or letters were used, a date-letter was often added in the course of the fifteenth or later centuries ; indeed it was the great number of different alphabets in use, and the confusion thereby created that at length occasioned the abolition of all date-letters in 1783, and the substitution of a new and peculiar mark for each place to which the year should be added. We might almost infer from this that some of the provincial guilds, following the example of Paris, had used no mark except an alphabetical letter.

This new town mark of 1783 is unfortunately no clue to any older one ; for it was in hardly any case an armorial bearing, but some quite modern and fanciful device. A long list of them is given by Lacroix, and, for what they are worth, they are reproduced at the end of this chapter ; though, as they were in use only from 1784 to 1789, five troublous years in which little plate could have been made, it must be confessed that they are of small interest.

The shield of arms, then, accompanied or not by a date-letter, or in some instances, perhaps, a date-letter only, was the usual town mark until 1784 ; and from

1784 to 1789 this new modern device, accompanied by
the last two figures of the year, or else some small,
secret, and variable character.

The South Kensington Museum Handbook on Gold
and Silver, disappointingly enough, tells us that in the
work of Lacroix will be found the arms and stamps of a
large number of old French provincial corporations ; unfortunately, this is only true of their arms, and the arms
of these guilds seem to be no clue at all to the hall-marks
used by them.   Neither the N E 'avec une hermine
cravatée' of ancient Nantes, or perhaps of Vannes near
Nantes, nor the bend of Strasbourg are even to be guessed
at from the arms given by Lacroix as those of the goldsmiths' guilds in those cities, nor from the devices
adopted by them in 1783.   The lamb and flag of Rouen
is a rare exception.

A better clue is to be found from 1672, owing to the
fact that from that time the mark of the farmer of the
duty, or *poinçon de charge*, should be found on provincial
French, as on Paris, plate in addition to the town-mark,
maker's mark, and date-letter.

This mark was the mint letter of the town, and at one
or other of the mint towns, of which there seem to have
been some twenty or thirty, probably one for each of the
provinces into which France was divided from the time
of Louis XIV., plate must have paid duty and received
the mark of the charge and discharge by way of receipt.

For the complete table of the marks, Parisian and provincial, in use during the administration of Fouache from
1774 to 1780, appended to this chapter, the author is
indebted to the kindness of a distinguished French
savant, the Baron Jerome Pichon, who is, without doubt,
the highest authority on these points.

This table gives the mint-letters of the towns that

were at that time centres of jurisdiction, but it will be remarked that some few letters of the alphabet are omitted.
If these are restored from other sources, we shall probably be in possession of a nearly complete list of all
the towns in France that have ever been of much plate-
making or plate-marking consequence.

These missing letters are F, Q, T, V, and W.

F is the letter for Angers, the mint at which place
was suppressed in 1738.

Q was used at Perpignan.

T once stood for Nantes.

V seems for some time (after 1690) to have been in
use at Amiens.

W used at Lille in some part of the eighteenth century.

To this list may be added a double B, which was in use
at Strasbourg as the double A was at Metz.

It would seem that no letter was used at Pau for the
province of Bearn ; possibly a cow was the local device
for that town.

Lastly, the letters MA, linked by being placed one
over the other, sometimes stand for Marseilles.

The fashion of the provincial mint letters used for the
poinçon de charge probably followed the Paris use ;
thus if the Paris A was accompanied by three fleurs-de-
lis, so probably were the provincial letters in use at the
same period.

We have appended, for the purpose of illustrating
this point, a fac-simile of an engraving given by M.
Raibaud of the marks in use in Paris and one or two
other large towns shortly before the abolition of taxes
in 1791, but it cannot be taken as an accurate repre-
sentation of the letters. It serves, however, to show
the sort of correspondence which was no doubt preserved
between the fashion of the Parisian and provincial Mint

letters of the *poinçon de charge*. The author has been
able to assign the charge and discharge marks for Grénoble found on a spoon made by one Fauche of that
place to the interval between 1762 and 1768, from
their obvious relationship to those used in Paris under
J. J. Prevost, the farmer-general of that date.

These tables, and one of the arms of the towns in which
plate was chiefly made, will be all that the amateur or
collector of old French plate will require to enable him to
identify the origin of almost any specimens of provincial
work older than 1784 that come under his notice.

It is not likely that any great amount of plate was
made anywhere but in Paris, at all events for the last
two centuries.

Some handsome eighteenth-century French plate was
sold at Messrs. Christie and Manson's, amongst "the
Gregory Heirlooms" in the summer of 1878, bearing
four marks, viz., maker's mark, a date-letter, a Roman
capital L, accompanied by a very small fleur-de-lis or
trefoil, being no doubt the duty mark for Bayonne, and
a fleur-de-lis, which was either the mark *de décharge*
or a town mark then used at Bayonne.

A few words must be added about the provincial
marks introduced in 1783 in lieu of those previously in
use.   It would have been better to give them in a
separate chapter but for the two facts that they, like the
earlier marks, are found in conjunction with the duty
marks, and that they only lasted for about six years.
If included, therefore, in the present chapter, French
hall-marking is carried down to the time of the abolition
of taxes, and with them of all old plate-marks, in 1791.

It has been a question whether the tables of these
marks, as given by Raibaud and Lacroix, should be engraved afresh for this handbook, or whether the names of

Silver-gilt and enamelled tazza and cover, set with garnets. Made by Morrel Freres, Paris 1857. Victoria & Albert Museum.

the towns, with a plain description of their marks, would
not be an almost better indication. The actual marks
used differ very much from the representations of them
as given in the mint tables ; besides which, though the
marks in the tables are called fixed and invariable, in
point of fact they all of them, including the letter P for
Paris, seem to have varied in design each year.

They are given, however, at the end of this chapter,
and as before remarked, for what they were worth. It
will be remembered that the mint letter of one or other
provincial jurisdiction should be found with them. This
may often serve to clear up any doubt as to the town
mark, by adding an indication of the local centre to
which it belonged.

In conclusion, as to the standards in use in the provinces of France. They were usually those of Paris, and
in the case of gold this is so almost without exception.
Burgundy and Lorraine, however, each had an inferior
standard of their own for silver, although recognising the
French standard as well.

That of Burgundy was 11 den. 8 grs. fine, with a
remedy of 2 gr., and was used at Besançon, Lille, and
other places. The silver standard of Lorraine was lower,
being only 9 den. 12 gr. fine, without any remedy. This
was worked at Nancy and Bar-le-Duc. Strasbourg too
had standards of its own ; 18½ carats for gold, with a
small remedy ; and 9 den. 20 grs., with a remedy of
2 grs., for silver.

The following tables are used thus :—

In Table I. will be found the towns arms. In
Table II. the mint letter of the *poinçon de charge* from
1672. Table III. will indicate the sort of comparison
which should be made between the provincial and the

Parisian mint letter in order to fix to which of the
farmers or administrators of the taxes it relates. Lastly,
Table IV. will give the town emblem which will be
found between 1783 and 1789 instead of an earlier
town mark, but still in conjunction with a mark of the
charge.

TABLE I.

ARMS OF FRENCH TOWNS WHERE PLATE WAS MADE BEFORE 1783.
THE TOWN OF JURISDICTION, THE MINT LETTER OF WHICH
WOULD, SINCE 1672, BE FOUND AS A MARK IN CONJUNCTION WITH
ANY OF THE FOLLOWING TOWN ARMS, IS GIVEN IN BRACKETS.

Abbeville (Amiens). Three bends within a bordure, on a chief three
fleurs-de-lis.*

Agen (Bordeaux). Party per pale, 1st, a griffin or eagle displayed,
holding in its claws a scroll; 2nd, a castle.

Alais (Montpellier). A wing.

Aix (Aix). Five pallets, a chief of Jerusalem, Sicily and Anjou.

Alençon (Caen). Semy of fleurs-de-lis, a bordure charged with ten
bezants.

Amiens (Amiens). Three branches, a chief of France.

Angers (Angers). A key in pale, on a chief two fleurs-de-lis.

Angoulême (Limoges). Semy of fleurs-de-lis, a bend compony gu. and
arg. Another coat is, a city gate of two towers, and in chief a fleur-de-
lis in a heart crowned.

Apt (Aix). A sheathed sword in pale, the girdle wound round the
scabbard.

Arles (Aix). A lion sejant, the right paw raised, the tail between the
legs.

Arras (Lille). On a fess three rats, a mitre in chief and two saltire
crosses in base. Another coat is, a lion having on his neck a shield
semy of fleurs-de-lis with a label of four points, each charged with three
towers.

Avalon (Dijon). A single tower.

Avesnes (Lille). Bendy of six gu. and or, above the shield a hive sur-
rounded by bees.

Aurillac (Riom). Three escallops, 2 and 1, on a chief 3 fleurs-de-lis.

Autun (Dijon). A lion rampant, a chief of ancient Burgundy, which
was three bends within a bordure. Another coat is a porcupine. A third
was, three serpents in form of circles, their tails in their mouths, on a
chief two lions' heads affrontées erased.

---

* The coats of arms in this list are not described in minute heraldic detail, but
only with a view to their identification when used as hall-marks.

Auxerre (Paris). Billety, over all a lion.

Bailleul (Lille). A cross vair, a lion in the first quarter.

Bar-le-Duc (Nancy). Semy of crosses-croslet fitchy, over all two fishes (bars) addorsed.

Bar-sur-Aube (Troyes). A bend, double cotised, potent and counter-potent.

Bayonne (Bayonne). A battlemented tower upon a wave, supported by two lions, one on each side, with their backs against two fir trees, a fleur-de-lis in chief between the two trees. Another coat is, a sword in pale, point downwards.

Beaucaire (Montpellier). Quarterly, or and gu.

Beaune (Dijon). A figure of Bellona upon a ground az., in right hand a sword, the left hand on the breast. After 1540. Our Lady leading the infant Jesus with her left hand, and holding a bunch of grapes in the right.

Beauvais (Paris). A pale fitchy.

Bergues St. Vinox (Lille). Party per pale, 1 a lion, 2 a fess, with a nail in base, on a canton a lion within a bordure.

Besançon (Besançon). An imperial eagle, holding in each of its claws two small columns.

Beziers (Montpellier). Three fesses, on a chief 3 fleurs-de-lis.

Blois (Orleans). A fleur-de-lis. Another coat is, a porcupine bearing a shield with a fleur-de-lis fronting a fox bearing a similar shield.

Bordeaux (Bordeaux). A castle surmounted by a lion passant, at the foot of the walls a river charged with a crescent, on a chief 3 fleurs-de-lis.

Boulogne-sur-Mer (Amiens). A swan. Another coat is, Party per pale, 1st, a swan; 2nd, 3 torteaux, 2 and 1.

Bourg en Bresse (Dijon). A cross botonée.

Bourges (Bourges). Three sheep passant within an engrailed bordure; on a chief 3 fleurs-de-lis.

Brest (Rennes). Party per pale, 1st, 3 fleurs-de-lis, 2nd, ermine. Another coat is, a ship; a chief ermine.

Caen (Caen). Party per fess, 3 fleurs-de-lis, 2 and 1.

Cahors (Toulouse). A bridge of five arches, on which are five towers.

Calais (Amiens). A fleur-de-lis crowned, supported by a crescent. Another coat is, a vessel with sail furled.

Cambrai (Lille). A double-headed eagle, charged with an escutcheon with 3 lions, 2 and 1.

Carcassonne (Perpignan). Semy of fleurs-de-lis, a castle of three towers.

Castres (Perpignan). Gules, 3 piles or, issuing from the dexter side.

Chalons-sur-Saone (Dijon). Three annulets, 2 and 1.

Chalons-sur-Marne (Reims). A cross between 4 fleurs-de-lis.

Charité, La (Bourges). Party per fess, in chief 3 towers, each surmounted by a fleur-de-lis, the base chequy.

Chartres (Paris). Three bezants, each charged with an antique letter and a fleur-de-lis, a chief with 3 fleurs-de-lis.

Chateau Gonthier (Angers). No arms found.

Chateau Thierry (Reims).   A castle of 5 towers between 3 fleurs-de-lis.
Chatellerault (Poitiers).   A lion rampant.
Chatillon sur Seine (Dijon).   A square castle with corner towers,
3 fleurs-de-lis ranged in chief.
Chaumont en Bassigny (Troyes).   Party per pale, 1st, a demy escarbuncle issuing from the sinister side, 2nd, a bend cotised; on a chief
3 fleurs-de-lis.
Clermont Ferrand (Riom).   A fimbriated cross between 4 fleurs-de-lis.
Cognac (La Rochelle).   Francis 1st on horseback, on a chief 3 fleurs-de-lis.
Colmar (Strasbourg).   Per pale gu. and vert, over all a spur rowel.
Compiègne (Paris).   A lion semy of fleurs-de-lis and crowned.
Coutances (Caen).   Three pillars in pale, on a chief a leopard.
Daligre (La Rochelle).   No arms found.
Dieppe (Rouen).   Per pale gu. and az., a 3-masted ship in full sail, or.
Dijon (Dijon).   Gu. a chief parted per pale, 1st, semy of fleurs-de-lis
within a bordure compony, 2nd, bendy of six within a bordure.
Dinan (Rennes).   A castle of 3 towers, on a chief a row of 5 ermine
spots.
Dole (Besançon).   Party per fess, in chief a lion issuing out of the
base, in base a sun.
Douai (Lille).   Gules.
Draguignan (Aix).   A wyvern.
Dunkerque (Lille).   Party per fess; in chief a lion passant, in base a
dolphin.
Etampes (Paris).   Three battlemented towers, the middle one charged
with an escutcheon bearing, quarterly, 1 and 4 a fleur-de-lis, 2 and 3 a
battlemented tower.
Falaise (Caen).   A castle of three towers.
Fécamp (Rouen).   No arms found.
Fère, La.   Barry of six vair and gu.
Fontenay le Comte (Poitiers).   A fountain ; sometimes between 2 unicorns and with a fleur-de-lis in chief.
Gien (Orleans).   A castle with a pointed top, accompanied by two
towers also.
Gisors (Rouen).   A cross engrailed, on a chief 3 fleurs-de-lis.
Grasse (Aix).   A paschal lamb with flag.
Grénoble (Grénoble).   Three roses.
Guise (Reims).   Semy of fleurs-de-lis, a lion over all on the dexter side.
Havre, Le (Rouen).   A salamander crowned, on a chief 3 fleurs-de-lis.
Another coat is, a ship in full sail.
Joinville (Troyes).   Three breys (horses' bits) in fess, on a chief a lion
naissant.
Issoire (Riom).   A shake-fork, or letter Y, with a stem hooked to
dexter.
Issoudun (Bourges).   A shake-fork or letter Y between 3 fleurs-de-lis.
Landrecy (Lille).   Three bars couped.

Langheac (Riom).　Three pales vair.

Langres (Troyes).　A cross saltire between 4 fleurs-de-lis.

Laon (Reims).　Three martlets, on a chief 3 fleurs-de-lis.

Laval (Angers).　A lion passant guardant (? rampant).

Liesse, Notre Dame de (Reims).　No arms found.

Lille (Lille).　A fleur-de-lis.

Limoges (Limoges).　St. Martial, on a chief 3 fleurs-de-lis.

Lisieux (Caen).　Two keys in saltire, on a chief 3 fleurs-de-lis.

Longwy (Metz).　Az. a bend arg.

Lons le Saulnier (Besançon).　Quarterly, 1, a letter N under a star ; 2, a bend.　3, a heart.　4, or.

L'Orient (Nantes).　A ship sailing over sea, a sun rising behind mountains, a canton ermine, on a chief 3 bezants.

Loudon (Tours).　A tower ; on a chief 3 fleurs-de-lis.

Lunel (Montpellier).　A crescent.

Luçon (Poitiers).　Three fishes (pikes) placed fesswise.

Lyon (Lyon).　A lion, holding in his right paw a sword, on a chief 3 fleurs-de-lis.

Macon (Dijon).　Three annulets, 2 and 1.

Manosque (Aix).　Quarterly 1 and 4, a dexter hand, 2 and 3 the same.

Mans, Le (Tours).　A cross and 3 church candlesticks ; 2 and 1, a key in pale upon the lower one, on a chief 3 fleurs-de-lis.

Mantes (Paris).　Party per pale a fleur-de-lis and a branch of mint, conjoined and dimidiated.

Marennes (La Rochelle).　No arms found.

Marseilles (Aix).　Arg. a cross az.

Maubeuge (Lille).　Quarterly, 4 lions rampant.

Meaux (Paris).　Party per pale vert and gu., the Gothic capital letter M crowned, a chief semy of fleurs-de-lis.

Melle (Poitiers).　No arms found.

Melun (Paris).　Semy of fleurs-de-lis, a castle triple-towered.

Mende (Montpellier).　A sun in splendour, in chief a Gothic capital letter M in base.

Metz (Metz).　Party per pale, arg. and sa.

Mezières (Reims).　Two rakes (râteaux) in chief, a Roman capital letter M in base.

Milhau (Toulouse).　Three pales, a chief semy of fleurs-de-lis.

Montargis (Orleans).　The Roman capital letter M crowned between 3 fleurs-de-lis, the letters L and F in base, one on each side of the M and a little between it, the L on the dexter side.

Montauban (Toulouse).　A trunk of a dead tree ; on a chief 3 fleurs-de-lis.

Montpellier (Montpellier).　A shield charged with a torteau.

Morlaix (Rennes).　A ship on a wave having sails of ermine, and a flag bearing 3 fleurs-de-lis.

Moulins (Riom).　Three crosses moline, 2 and 1.

Nantes (Nantes).　A ship with ermine sails ; on a chief a line of 7 ermine spots.

Narbonne (Perpignan). A key in pale, wards upwards, and a double cross ranged side by side in fess ; on a chief 3 fleurs-de-lis.

Nevers (Bourges). Billety, a lion rampant.

Nimes (Montpellier). A palm tree on a terrace, with a crocodile in fess chained, with the letters COL. NEM.

Niort (Poitiers). Semy of fleurs-de-lis, a tower with its base in waves.

Noyon (Amiens). Arg. a fess gu.

Orléans (Orléans). Three flint-stones (cailloux) in a heart of fleurs-de-lis, 2 and 1 ; on a chief 3 fleurs-de-lis.

Parthenay (Poitiers). Barry, a bend engrailed.

Pau. Three stakes or pales united by a fess, on the middle one a peacock in his pride, 2 cows affrontées in base.

Payrat (Toulouse). No arms found.

Perigueux (Bordeaux). A castle of 3 towers, the middle one surmounted by a fleur-de-lis.

Perpignan (Perpignan). Two towers side by side, between them in chief a fleur-de-lis.

Pezenas (Montpellier). Barry, on a canton a porpoise embowed, on a chief 3 fleurs-de-lis.

Poitiers (Poitiers). A lion within a bordure charged with 12 bezants ; in a chief 3 fleurs-de-lis.

Pons en Saintonge (La Rochelle). A fess bendy of six, or and gu.

Pontoise (Paris). A bridge of 4 arches supporting a tower having a turret ; 2 fleurs-de-lis in chief.

Provins (Paris). A castle of three towers and a central turret surmounted by a fleur-de-lis.

Puy en Velay (Riom). Semy of fleurs-de-lis, an eagle displayed.

Quimper (Nantes). A hart trippant, on a chief 3 fleurs-de-lis.

Reims (Reims). Two branches entwined, a chief semy of fleurs-de-lis.

Rennes (Rennes). Paley of 6 arg. and sable, on a chief 3 fleurs-de-lis.

Réthel (Reims). Two rakes without handles, one above another.

Riez (Aix). An apple tree with a bear erect, reaching the apples.

Riom (Riom). Two fleurs-de-lis in chief ; the Roman capital letter R in base.

Rochefort (La Rochelle). A rock under a fleur-de-lis in chief.

Rochelle, La (La Rochelle). A ship in full sail ; sometimes with a chief of 3 fleurs-de-lis.

Rodez (Toulouse). Three annulets ; on a chief 3 fleurs-de-lis.

Rouen (Rouen). A lamb and flag ; on a chief 3 fleurs-de-lis.

Sables, Les (Poitiers). No arms found.

Saintes (La Rochelle). A castle with 5 lofty towers, its base in water.

St. Esprit (Montpellier). No arms found.

St. Flour (Riom). Paly gu. and or.

St. Germain-en-Laye (Paris). A child's berceaunette with a fleur-de-lis in chief and 1638 in base.

St. Jean d'Angely (La Rochelle). Semy of fleurs-de-lis, a head of John the Baptist in a dish on high stand.

St. Lo (Caen). A unicorn passant ; on a chief 3 fleurs-de-lis.

St. Malo (Rennes). A portcullis ; in chief a greyhound courant.
St. Maixent (Poitiers). A crown ; on a chief 3 fleurs-de-lis.
St. Martin (La Rochelle). No arms found.
St. Menehould (Reims). Three crescents entwined.
St. Omer (Lille). A double cross (of Lorraine).
St. Quentin (Amiens). A man's head affrontée, behind it 2 batons between three fleurs-de-lis.
Salins (Besançon). Or, a bend gu.
Saumur (Angers). A fess embattled between 3 fleurs de-lis in chief and the Roman capital letter S in base.
Sedan (Metz). A boar passant under a tree.
Semur en Auxois (Dijon). A tower charged with a shield bendy.
Senlis (Paris). Gu. a pale or.
Sens (Paris). Semy of fleurs-de-lis, a tower.
Soissons (Reims). A fleur-de-lis.
Strasbourg (Strasbourg). Arg. a bend gu.
Tarascon (Aix). A castle of 3 towers, beneath it a dragon devouring a man.
Thouars (Poitiers). Three bunches of grapes.
Toul (Metz). A capital letter T.
Toulon (Aix). Or, a cross az., a flag in the first quarter, a chief semy of fleurs-de-lis.
Toulouse (Toulouse). A lamb supporting an upright rod surmounted by a fleur-de-lis, between 2 castles, a chief semy of fleurs-de-lis.
Tours (Tours). Three towers, 2 and 1, on a chief 3 fleurs-de-lis. Another coat is, a tower between 2 fleurs-de-lis, one on each side.
Trévoux (Lyon). A tower ; on a chief 3 fleurs-de-lis, each charged with a bend.
Troyes (Troyes). A bend cotised potent and counter potent; on a chief 3 fleurs-de- lis.
Uzes (Montpellier). Bendy, or and gu. Another coat is, three fesses ; on a chief 3 fleurs-de-lis.
Valenciennes (Lille). Party per pale, 1 a lion rampant, 2 a swan. Another coat is, 2 lions leopardies one above another.
Valognes (Caen). A lion passant guardant.
Vannes (Nantes). An ermine courant, his head crowned and with a flying scarf or cravat (écharpe) arg. semy of ermine round the neck.
Verdun (Metz). A fleur-de-lis under a royal crown.
Versailles (Paris). Three fleurs-de-lis ; on a chief a demi eagle with 2 heads, each crowned.
Vesoul (Besançon). Party per fess, the chief billety, a demy lion issuing out of the fess, in the base a crescent.
Vigan, Le. No arms found.
Vitry-le-Français (Troyes). A salamander crowned, in chief two Roman capital letters F, each crowned.

TABLE II.

TABLEAU GÉNÉRAL DES DÉNOMINATIONS ET FIGURES DES POINÇONS DE LA MARQUE D'OR ET D'ARGENT DE LA RÉGIE DE JN. BTE. FOUACHE (1774–1780).

Généralités.

Charge des gros ouvr.	Charge des ouvr. d'or et menus ouvr. d'ar.	Décharge des gros ouvr.	Décharge des ouvr. d'or et menus ouvr d'ar.
Paris. A	chiffre des 5 lettres, Paris	tête de bœuf	tête de singe.
Rouen. B	chiffre des initiales syllabaires,* RE	poids de marc	coquille de noix avec portion de fruit.
Caen, Alençon. C	" CE	tête de Socrate	un autel d'amitié.
Lyon. D	ch. des 4 lettres, Lyon	une oreille humaine	tête de cheval.
Tours. E	" 5 lettres, Tours	un pied droit, vu par dessous	tête de hibou.
Poitiers. G	ch. des initiales syll. PT	un chat	tête de bouc.
La Rochelle. H	ch. des initiales, LR	un écureuil	tête de vache.
Limoges. I	ch. des init. syll. LM	vase antique à 2 anses	chapeau d'évêque.
Bordeaux. K	" BD	couronne impériale	un masque de profil.
Bayonne, Auch. L	" BON	une gibicière	pied droit, vu par dessous.
Toulouse, Montauban. M	" TLS	feuille de vigne	une mauviette.
Montpellier. N	" MPL	2 branches de laurierliées ensemble	tête de pavot.
Riom. O	" RO	pied gauche, vu de $\frac{3}{4}$	bonnet à la turque.
Dijon. P	" DJ	coquille marine	chapeau de jardinier.
Moulins, Orleans. R	" OLA	main gauche fermée	tête d'écureuil.
Chalons. S	ch. des init. et fin. RS (*sic*)	épi de blé	crosse de pistolet.
Amiens, Soissons. X	ch. des init. syll. AM	une tête d'ours	tête de vieillard.

* Syllabaires, initiales des syllabes composant le nom.

TABLE II.—*continued.*

Charge des gros ouvr.	Charge des ouvr. d'or et menus ouvr. d'ar.	Décharge des gros ouvr.	Décharge des ouvr. d'or et menus d'ar.
Bourges. **Y**	ch. des init. syll. **BG** . .	main droite à demi-fermée	tête de mouton.
Grenoble. **Z** . . .	„ „ **GNB** .	patte droite de devant de lion	casque de profil.
Aix. **&**	ch. des init. et fin. **AX** .	chapiteau d'ordre composite	tête de cygne.
Rennes. 9 . . .	ch. des init. syll. **RN** .	branche de laurier et de palme	nœud de ruban.
Metz. **AA** . . .	ch. des init. et fin. **MZ** .	tête de biche	tête d'amour.

POINÇONS GÉNÉRAUX.

Contremarque ;—une pantoufle d'homme.
Ouvrages venant de l'étranger ;—un pied humain gauche, vu de ¾.
Reconnaissance ;—culasse de canon.
Ouvrages vieux ;—tête de levrette.
Très-petits ouvrages ;—graine de mouron.

POINÇONS PARTICULIERS À LA VILLE DE PARIS.

Ouvrages allant à l'étranger ;—tête de chameau.
Gratis (pour ouvrages marqués gratis) ;—couronne royale.

TABLE III.

SPECIMENS OF THE MARKS OF THE CHARGE AND DISCHARGE AS USED
IN PARIS AND THE THREE CHIEF TOWNS IN THE PROVINCES
SHORTLY BEFORE THE ABOLITION OF ALL TAXES IN 1791. (AFTER
RAIBAUD.)

	CHARGE.		DISCHARGE.			
	Large silver.	Gold and small silver.	Large silver.	Gold and small silver.		
Paris.					Ingots for drawing.	
Lyons.					Foreign work.	
Bordeaux.					Old work.	
Rouen.					Very small wares.	

Silver candlestick with the mark of Daniel Coppin and the Paris mark for 1723. Height 20.5 cm. Victoria & Albert Museum.

TABLE IV.

A TABLE OF THE MARKS USED BY THE COMMUNITIES OF GOLDSMITHS IN THE PROVINCIAL TOWNS OF FRANCE FROM MAY, 1784, UNTIL 1789 (AFTER THE PLATES PUBLISHED IN 1786 BY BERNIER, ENGRAVER TO THE MINT), TAKEN FROM "TRAITÉ DE LA GARANTIE," ETC. PAR B. L. RAIBAUD, AND "HISTOIRE DE L'ORFÈVRERIE," ETC., PAR LACROIX ET SERÉ.

MARK.		TOWN.	JURISDICTION OF
A bee.		Abbeville, 1508* . .	Amiens.†
The hands of a clock.		Agen, 1775 . . .	Bordeaux.
A wing.		Alais, 1775 . . .	Montpellier.
A wheatsheaf.		Aix	Aix.
A spider.		Alençon, 1718 . .	Caen.
A crossbow.		Amiens, 1727 . . .	Amiens.
A battledore.		Angers	Angers.
A calf's head.		Angoulême, 1719 . .	Limoges.

* The date given is that of the incorporation of the goldsmiths of each place into a regular Community.

† The Mint-letter or *poinçon de charge* found on any piece of provincial plate will be that of the local centre of jurisdiction, under one or other of which each town was placed. For these letters refer to the preceding Table (p. 62).

F

TABLE IV.—*continued.*

MARK.		TOWN.	JURISDICTION OF
A hand-brush or sprinkler.		Annonay . . .	Montpellier.
A pair of scales.		Apt	Aix.
A crozier head.		Arles	Aix.
A chair.		Arras, 15— . . .	Lille.
A cow's head.		Avalon, 1743. . .	Dijon.
A shovel.		Avesnes, 1773 . . .	Lille.
A jackboot.		Aurillac . . .	Riom.
A buckle.		Autun, 1784 . . .	Dijon.
A flat candlestick.		Auxerre, 1731 `. .	Paris.
A compass card in flat square case.		Bailleul, 1731 . . .	Lille.
A fish and a flower.		Bar-le-Duc* . . .	Nancy.
An heraldic maunche.		Bar-sur-Aube, 1763 . .	Troyes.

* The goldsmiths of Bar-le-Duc used 2 marks :—1. For Paris standard, two barbels back to back, crowned. 2. For Lorraine standard, 3 pansies, 2 and 1, crowned.—*Lacroix.*

TABLE IV.—*continued.*

MARK.		TOWN.	JURISDICTION OF
A birdcage.		Bayonne,* 1512 . .	Bayonne.
A cafetière.		Beaucaire, 1776 . .	Montpellier.
A wine-glass.		Beaune, 1742 . .	Dijon.
A fish.		Beauvais, 1609 . . .	Paris.
A seal.		Bergues St. Vinox, 1750	Lille.
A corkscrew.		Besançon,† 1688 . .	Besançon.
A trumpet.		Béziers, 1598 . . .	Montpellier.
A two-handled vase with cover.		Blois, 1567 . . .	Orléans.
An unicorn.		Bordeaux, 12— . .	Bordeaux.
A sailor's hat.		Boulogne - sur - Mer et Montreuil, 1744	Amiens.
A double chain with tassel end.		Bourg-en-Bresse, 1747 .	Dijon.
A horned sheep's head.		Bourges, 1557 . .	Bourges.

* For a second mark, the town arms.—*Lacroix.*

† An additional mark *de reconnaissance* was used here of 2 C's back to back, ƆƆ, surmounted by a fleur-de-lis.—*Lacroix.*

TABLE IV.—*continued.*

MARK.		TOWN.	JURISDICTION OF
A great ship.		Brest, Lesneven Lander-neau, 1695	Rennes.
A ploughshare.		Caen, 1594 . . .	Caen.
A hound sejant.		Cahors, 1777 . . .	Toulouse.
A spur.		Calais, 1748 . . .	Amiens.
A horse's head.		Cambrai, 1315 . .	Lille.
A ciborium or covered cup.		Carcassonne, 1676 . .	Perpignan.
A small bell.		Castres, 1749 . . .	Perpignan.
A leopard or lioness passant.		Cau de bec . . .	Rouen.
A key.		Chalons-sur-Saone, 1682	Dijon.
A watch-key.		Chalons-sur-Marne, 1749	Reims.
A bird soaring.		Chartres, 15— . .	Paris.
A pair of com-passes.		Chateau Gonthier, 1757	Angers.
A cock.		Chateau Thierry . .	Reims.

TABLE IV.—*continued.*

MARK.		TOWN.	JURISDICTION OF
A pen-knife.		Chatellerault, 1758 .	Poitiers.
A single tower.		Chatillon-sur-Seine, 15—	Dijon.
A crescent moon with face in profile enclosed.		Chaumont-en-Bassigny, 1744	Troyes.
A tree.		Clermont Ferrand, 15--	Riom.
A barbed spear-head.		Cognac, 1762 . . .	La Rochelle.
A left-hand glove.		Colmar	Strasbourg.
A stag's head.		Compiègne, 1667 . .	Paris.
An inkstand.		Coutances, 1751 . .	Caen.
A bowl with two flat handles.		Daligre ci-devant Marans, 1758	La Rochelle.
A fish.		Dieppe, 1599 . . .	Rouen.
A globe on a stand.		Dijon, 15— . . .	Dijon.
An anchor.		Dinan, 1746 . . .	Rennes.
A funnel.		Dole *	Besançon.

* Also 2 C's back to back, ƆC, surmounted by a ducal coronet, cf. Besançon.— *Lacroix.*

TABLE IV.—*continued.*

MARK.		TOWN.	JURISDICTION OF
A . . . . with crown above and crossed branches below.		Douai	Lille.
An ear of wheat.		Draguignan, 1751 . .	Aix.
A ragged branch.		Dunkerque, 1753 . .	Lille.
A crayfish.		Etampes . . .	Paris.
A lancet.		Falaise, 1750 . . .	Caen.
A stirrup.		Fécamp, 1745 . .	Rouen.
A torch.		Fontenay-le-Comte, 1571	Poitiers.
An arrow.		Gien, 1757 . . .	Orléans.
A sprig of yew.		Gisors, 1754 . . .	Rouen.
A fork.		Grasse	Aix.
A dolphin.		Grenoble . . .	Grenoble.
The head of a pole or staff.		Guise and Vervins, 1743	Reims.
A lance with a pennon.		Havre, Le, 15— . .	Rouen.

TABLE IV.—*continued.*

MARK.		TOWN.	JURISDICTION OF
A staff with small flag, or guidon.		Joinville, 1757 . .	Troyes.
An oak sprig with acorn.		Issoire, 1766 . . .	Riom.
A goblet.		Issoudun, 1757 . .	Bourges.
A holy-water sprinkler.		La Charité, 1757 . .	Bourges.
A pink.		La Fère . . .	Reims.
A scalpel.		Landrecy, 1779 . .	Lille.
A rule or level.		Langheac, 1784 . .	Riom.
A clasp-knife open.		Langres, 1566 . . .	Troyes.
A prickly arti-choke.		Laon	Reims.
A griffin rampant.		La Rochelle, 1698 . .	La Rochelle.
A frog.		Laval	Angers.
A gridiron.		Le Vigan, 1775 . .	Montpellier.
A hatchet.		Liesse, Notre Dame de, 1749	Reims.

TABLE IV.—*continued.*

MARK.		TOWN.	JURISDICTION OF
A flying bird.		Lille	Lille.
A peasant's wood-basket.		Limoges, 1719 . . .	Limoges.
A cornucopia.		Lisieux, 1750 . .	Caen.
An heraldic label.		Longwy	Metz.
A Roman lamp.		Lons-le-Saulnier, 1780 .	Besançon.
A five-pointed star with three flames issuing from it.		Lorient, 1745 . .	Nantes.
A lantern.		Loudun, 1646 . . .	Tours.
A pine cone.		Lunel, 1775 . . .	Montpellier.
A shuttle.		Luçon, 1758 . . .	Poitiers.
		Lunéville.*	
A lion's head.		Lyon	Lyon.
An open right right.		Macon, 1600 . . .	Dijon.

* For Paris standard, a letter C crowned. For Lorraine standard, a letter C crowned, but in the middle of it a cross of Lorraine. The goldsmiths of this place and its dependencies used the two initial letters of their name, and a particular device for the town they lived in—*e.g.*, for Lunéville, a crescent; for Charmes, a greyhound ; for Epinal, a star ; for Rembervillers, a letter R ; and for Saint Diez, a rose.—*Lacroix.*

TABLE IV.—*continued.*

MARK.		TOWN.	JURISDICTION OF
A closed book.		Manosque	Aix.
A tulip flower.		Mans, Le, 1757 . .	Tours.
A mascle, the piercing invected.		Mantes	Paris.
An oyster.		Marennes, 1777 . .	La Rochelle.
A riband tied in a bow.		Marseille, 12—. . .	Aix.
An eye.		Maubeuge . . .	Lille.
A cat sitting.		Méaux	Paris.
A left ear.		Melle	Poitiers.
An eel.		Melun, 1727 . . .	Paris.
A butterfly.		Mende, 1757 . . .	Montpellier.
A cannon.		Mézières, 1746 . .	Reims.
A peacock in his pride.		Metz, 1635 . . .	Metz.
A fritillary flower.		Milhau, 1770 . .	Toulouse.

TABLE IV.—*continued.*

MARK.		TOWN.		JURISDICTION OF
A comb.		Montargis, 1737 . .		Orléans.
A steel-yard.		Montauban, 1705 . .		Toulouse.
A still.		Montpellier . . .		Montpellier.
A square column.		Morlaix, 1607 . .		Rennes.
The sails of a windmill.		Moulins, 1736 . . .		Riom.
. . . . .	. . .	Nancy * . . .		Nancy.
A tilting spear.		Nantes, 1579 . .		Nantes.
A tobacco-pipe.		Narbonne, 1669 . .		Perpignan.
A wine-bottle.		Nevers, 1757 . .		Bourges.
A porcupine.		Nimes, 1586 . . .		Montpellier.

* Two standards used here :—1. Paris, marked with an A under an eagle crowned. 2. Lorraine, marked with the letter A under a cross of Lorraine. The goldsmiths of this community and its dependencies used the two initial letters of their names added to a special device for the town they lived in, as follows :—For Nancy, a thistle ; for Briey, a B ; for Commercy, a crown of roses ; for Etain, a pitcher ; for Mirecourt, an ermine ; for Neuf-château, a tower ; for Pont-à-Mousson, a heart ; for St. Mihiel, a balance ; for St. Nicholas, a spur-rowel ; for Vezelize, a lozenge ; for Bouquenom, a goat ; for Dieuze, an ear of wheat ; for Forbach, a pine cone ; for St. Avold, a pigeon ; and for Sarreguemines, an acorn.—*Lacroix.*

TABLE IV.—*continued.*

MARK.		TOWN.	JURISDICTION OF
A pot with one handle on three small feet.		Niort, 15— . . .	Poitiers.
A shallow oval pan or saltcellar.		Noyon, 1748 . . .	Amiens.
A Joan of Arc head with head-dress of feathers.		Orléans, 1611 . . .	Orléans.
Letter P crowned.		Paris, 1260 . . .	Paris.
A skate fish.		Parthenay, 1745 . .	Poitiers.
A cow.		Pau	Pau.
A pear with a leaf attached.		Payrat, Ste. Colombe et Chalabre, 1753	Toulouse.
A snail.		Perigueux . . .	Bordeaux.
A rat.		Perpignan . . .	Perpignan.
A garden rake.		Pézénas, 1586 . . .	Montpellier.
An Eastern cap with upright feather and jewel.		Poitiers	Poitiers.
A beehive.		Pons-en-Saintonge, 1785	La Rochelle.
A clove pink.		Pontoise, 1752 . . .	Paris.

TABLE IV.—*continued.*

MARK.		TOWN.	JURISDICTION OF
A moss-rose.		Provins, 1759 . .	Paris.
A pulley and rope.		Puy-en-Velay, 1367 . .	Riom.
A frame saw.		Quimper, 1780 . .	Nantes.
A bunch of grapes.		Reims, 1560 . . .	Reims.
A monkey sejant.		Rennes, 1579 . .	Rennes.
A quiver of arrows.		Réthel, 1660 . . .	Reims.
A saucer with one handle.		Riez	Aix.
A cross moline with an annulet.		Riom	Riom.
A rock.		Rochefort, 1713 . .	La Rochelle.
An urn or vase and RODEZ.		Rodez, 1777 . . .	Toulouse.
A branch with cluster of apples.		Rouen, 13— . . .	Rouen.
A sheep passant.		Sables, Les, 168— . .	Poitiers.
A spring clasp.		Saintes, 1758 . . .	La Rochelle.

TABLE IV.—*continued.*

MARK.		TOWN.	JURISDICTION OF
A magpie.		St. Esprit et Bagnols, 1777	Montpellier.
A squirrel sejant.		St. Flour, 1785 . . .	Riom.
A necklace.		St. Germain-en-Laye .	Paris.
A tooth with three fangs.		St. Jean d'Angely, 1779	La Rochelle.
A knotted club.		St. Lô	Caen.
A hammer.		St. Malo, 168— . .	Rennes.
A fly.		St. Meixent . . .	Poitiers.
A pair of snuffers.		St. Martin, 1785 . .	La Rochelle.
A watering-pot.		St. Menehould, 1742 .	Reims.
A dog passant.		St. Omer . . .	Lille.
A sword hilt.		St. Quentin et Péronne, 1748	Amiens.
A boar.		Salins, 1640 . . .	Besançon.
A helmet cup or ewer.		Saumur, 1749 . . .	Angers.

TABLE IV.—*continued*.

MARK.		TOWN.	JURISDICTION OF
A sun or head of Apollo in splendour.		Sedan, 1575 . . .	Metz.
A caduceus.		Semur-en-Auxois, 1701	Dijon.
A kidney bean.		Senlis	Paris.
A morion affrontée with feathers.		Sens, 1745 . . .	Paris.
A helmet affrontée with vizor closed.		Soissons, 1734 . . .	Reims.
A pear.		Strasbourg . . .	Strasbourg.
An open pair of scissors.		Tarascon	Aix.
A head of Mercury.		Thouars, 1714 . .	Poitiers.
A Moor's head.		Toul, 1643 . . .	Metz.
An ancient chariot.		Toulon, 1712 . . .	Aix.
A trowel.		Toulouse, 1500 . . .	Toulouse.
A parrot.		Tours, 1529 . . .	Tours.
A vine leaf.		Trévoux, 1783 . . .	Lyon.

TABLE IV.—*continued.*

MARK.		TOWN.	JURISDICTION OF
A bobbin handle or short staff.		Troyes, 1369 . . .	Troyes.
A marigold.		Valenciennes, 1625 . .	Lille.
An Apollo's head.		Valognes, 1750 . .	Caen.
An almond pod split open.		Vannes, 1745 . . .	Nantes.
A fleur de lys.		Verdun, 1630 . . .	Metz.
A wolf's head.		Versailles, 1768 . .	Paris.
A double fan.		Vesoul, 1775 . . .	Besançon.
A head with three-cornered hat and pigtail.		Vitry-le-Français, 1614	Troyes.

CHAPTER IV.

THE HALL MARKS USED IN PARIS AND THE DEPARTMENTS, SINCE 1797.

The modern hall-marks of 1791, 1809, 1819, and 1838, with tables.

THE two preceding Chapters have brought down the history of plate-marking in Paris and the Provinces of France respectively to the year 1789. From that time a period of blank chaos intervenes, until in 1797 the necessary step was taken of starting the craft afresh upon a modern basis. Possibly it was found difficult to get on any longer without taxes.

This new departure was effected by the law of 19 Brumaire, Year VI. (9 Nov. 1797), which is not without some importance, as it is the groundwork of all more modern French and Swiss legislation.

But for this fact and for the necessity of bringing our account of French marks down, somehow or other, to the present day, it would hardly be worth venturing into the bewildering sea of modern French hall-marks, since they are of comparatively little interest to amateur or collector, and of none to the antiquary.

A few words about such features of the law of 1797 as seem of any importance.

Its first chapter deals with the standards and remedy, which it appoints shall be those detailed on an earlier page. It also ordains that the quality of metal shall be for the future reckoned in millièmes.

The second chapter deals with the punches and marks.*

To those of the maker, of the standard, and of the office, it added stamps for ancient and foreign and plated wares, and also a special mark called the *poinçon de recense*, to be applied by public authority should it be necessary at any time to counteract the effect of any falsifications of standards or punches, by verifying the authenticity of the marks found upon plate. The punches in use up to this time were to be defaced as soon as the new punches were ready to replace them.

The mark of the maker was to consist of the initial letters of his name with a symbol, and was to be of the form and proportions ordained by the administration of the Mint. The Mint authorities in due course (17 Nivôse, an 6, or 6 Jan. 1797-8), prescribed that the maker's mark should be the initials of his name with a symbol in a lozenge. The punch of the standard was to be a cock, with Arabic figures 1, 2, or 3, to denote the various standards. These punches were to be uniform throughout the Republic.

A particular sign or number is added to the punch for each departmental office. A small punch of a cock's head was appointed for small gold wares, and a fasces for small wares of silver.

A punch for old plate alone, called *de hazard*, represented a hatchet; and plate coming from abroad was marked E T.

It then provided for the care of the punches, for the punishment of those who made false punches, and for the destruction of the punches previously in use.

---

* An entirely new set of marks were provided, which the tables appended to this Chapter sufficiently illustrate.

G

The third chapter levied a duty on gold and silver wares, whether made in France or imported, the usual exceptions being made in favour of the plate of ambassadors, and of a small quantity (5 hectogrammes) for travellers' personal use.

Other chapters then provide for the suppression of the Common Halls of Goldsmiths, the regulation of the Assay Offices and the functions of their officers; after which the obligations of makers are dealt with.

Goldsmiths were to enter their punches with the proper administrations, who were to strike them upon a copper plate kept for the purpose; they were to keep a detailed register of articles sold, and to particularise in the account rendered to customers the kind, standard, and weight of the articles, distinguishing between new and old wares.

These are all the provisions that are of any moment to us.

A few words need be added about the gratuitous *recense*, or verification, that accompanied the changes in the marks from time to time.

These took place in 1797, 1809, 1819, and lastly 1838, besides one for watches alone, in 1822. On the first occasion makers and merchants were bound, within six months after the publication of the law (Nov. 1797), to carry to the Assay Office of their district their new works of gold, silver, and silver gilt, marked with the old punches, to be marked with the punch of verification to be appointed by the Administration of the Mint. This verification of the old punches was to be done without charge for six months, but objects submitted after the expiration of that time were to be assayed and the assay dues charged.

Other unsold works, not bearing the stamp of the

Cup and cover, silver, with the mark of L.G. Thevénot and the Paris mark for 1750 – 1756. Height 17.7 cm.

poinçon de charge, were also to be brought in and stamped with the standard and assay marks, and assay dues to be paid upon them.

The verification mark was also applied on occasion of each subsequent recense *gratis* within a certain limit of time, as a counter-mark of verification to the marks of the set of punches whose use ceased on the day of the recense commencing, and it was applied to all wares then exposed for sale. After the limit of grace, all wares for sale marked with the old punches, but not thus verified, were liable to be assayed afresh and to a payment of duty. The marks used on each occasion will be found with the rest in the subjoined tables.

The last recense took place in 1838, and from that time the punches then ordained for the future have remained in use.

The tables of these complicated nineteenth-century marks have been published and are comparatively well known.

Those from 1797 to 1838 are given by M. Raibaud in great detail in a work called *Traité sur la Garantie des Matières d'Or et d'Argent,* published in Paris in 1825, whilst those of 1838 have been printed by Raibaud and also in a little treatise by De Geneste called *Nouveau Manuel de la Garantie, etc.,* published in Paris in 1839. Raibaud was assay master at Marseilles for many years, and De Geneste was *contrôleur de la garantie* for Paris in the year 1838. With these and other unexceptionable authorities, the following tables have been carefully compared. They are not of much interest to the antiquary or collector of old plate, but they are the only ones that have ever been printed in France or in England.

It is much to be regretted that some French antiquary with better opportunities than those at the disposal of a foreign amateur, should not, ere this, have given us means of dating the beautiful work of the French goldsmiths of the eighteenth century.

In the meanwhile, the foreign amateur deprecates hard measure for the imperfections incidental to a first attempt to furnish a key to the marks that will be found on all that remains of old Paris and provincial French plate.

SUMMARY OF MODERN MARKS AND EXPLANATION OF THE FOLLOWING TABLES.

1797–1809.

The cock in various attitudes for all the standards, accompanied by numerals to denote the qualities, alike for Paris and Departments. The numeral in the case of the Departments is in a different part of the punch, the attitude of the bird being the same for the same quality both in Paris and the Departments. A different attitude is adopted for each different quality.

The departmental assay mark is the classical head affrontée with the number of the Department.

Plate for sale, but not sold at the date of the commencement of these marks, if already marked with the then existing or older marks, would be countermarked or verified with the head having a Phrygian cap.

1809–1819.

The cock, but in a fresh set of attitudes, for standard; with a lion's head for Paris assay mark, or a hand with departmental number for the Departments, for gold.

The Paris, as well as the departmental marks for silver, are human heads, a number being added on the rim of the punch for the Departments; for smaller wares there is a different head, with the number on the cap for the Departments.

As before there are verification marks, used as in 1797.

1819–1838.

Four-footed animals are now appointed for standard, with numerals as before for gold; human heads for silver, as shown in the tables.

For assay and verification, various marks; the assay marks for the Departments being differenced with departmental number as before.

Verification marks used as before in 1797.

For very small wares of this period, see the table of Divisional Punches, and the long appended list of letters and figures that went with them.

The Bigornes are given on a separate plate. These were small countermarks introduced for the first time in 1819, and were applied in a novel manner, being borne on the surface of the anvil, and appearing, therefore, exactly behind the mark of the punch on the piece of plate under manipulation.

1838 to the present time.

For standard, head of Greek physician for gold, with departmental mark for each Department, as shown on appended table; for silver, head of Minerva, similarly differenced.

For assay, verification, etc., the various marks shown.

A new mark for gold chains, called the *poinçon de remarque*, was introduced at this time. It should appear at every *decimètre* of their length. A *decimètre* is a very little less than four inches.

As before, there were a great variety of Bigorne countermarks; those used in Paris are insects in profile, those of the Departments seen from above in bird's-eye view. It would be useless, if not impossible, to give engravings of them.

TABLE OF THE PUNCHES MADE IN PURSUANCE OF THE LAW OF 19
BRUMAIRE, YEAR VI. (9 NOV. 1797), TO REPLACE THOSE OF THE
COMMUNITIES OF GOLDSMITHS AND OF THE ADMINISTRATION OF
TAXES. USED 9 NOV. 1797—1 SEPT. 1809.

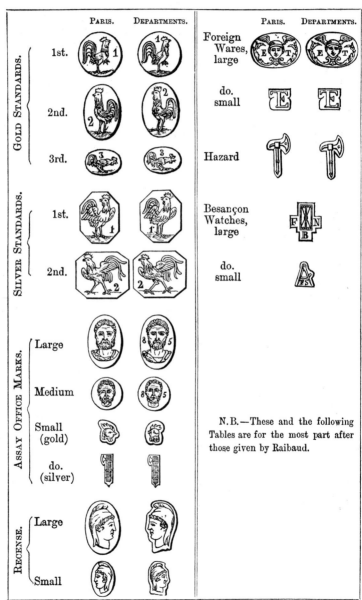

N.B.—These and the following
Tables are for the most part after
those given by Raibaud.

TABLE OF THE PUNCHES MADE IN PURSUANCE OF A DECREE OF 11 PRAIRIAL, YEAR XI. (31 MAY, 1803). USED 1 SEPT. 1809—16 AUG. 1819.

TABLE OF THE PUNCHES MADE IN PURSUANCE OF A ROYAL ORDINANCE
OF 22 OCT. 1817. USED 16 AUG. 1819—10 MAY, 1838.

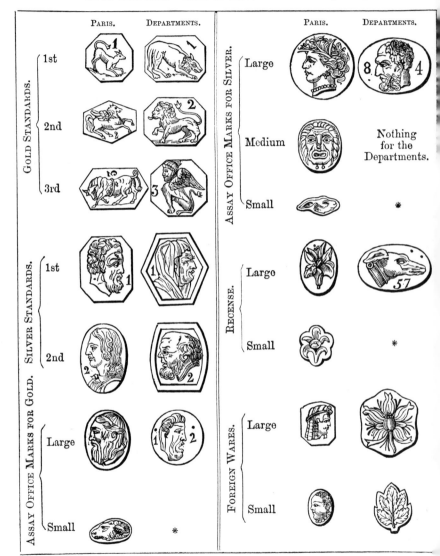

NOTE (1).—In the figure of the large Assay Office and Recense Marks is engraved
the number of the Department, as given in the following list of Assay Offices (p. 91).

(2.) For the marks proper to the spaces marked above with an asterisk, thus *, see
the Table of Divisional Punches on the opposite page.

TABLE OF DIVISIONAL PUNCHES MADE IN PURSUANCE OF THE ORDINANCE
OF 22 OCT. 1817. USED 16 AUG. 1819—10 MAY, 1838.

DIVISIONS.	GOLD.	SILVER.	RECENSE.
1. NORTH.	Car	Butterfly	Coffee Pot
2. NORTH-EAST.	Sword-hilt	Tortoise	Tower
3. EAST.	Tiara	Shell	Ciborium
4. SOUTH-EAST.	Fan	Beetle	Goblet
5. SOUTH.	Helmet	Lysse	Bell
6. SOUTH-WEST.	Lyre	Frog	Watering Pot
7. WEST.	Morion	Snail	Ewer
8. NORTH-WEST.	Trumpet	Skate-fish	Guitar
9. CENTRE.	Fleur-de-lis	Guinea Pig	Book

NOTE.—In the figure of the small Assay Office and Recense Marks for each Division is engraved the characteristic sign indicated in the following Tabular List of Assay Offices (p. 91).

TABLE OF THE SIGNS WHICH FORM THE BIGORNE MARKS AND COUNTER-
MARKS MADE IN PURSUANCE OF THE ORDINANCE OF 1 JULY,
1818. USED 16 AUG. 1819—10 MAY, 1838.

LARGE COUNTERMARK.		SMALL COUNTERMARK.	
Paris and Depart- ments.		Paris and Depart- ments.	
		Paris only.	
do.		do.	
do.		Departments only.	
do.		do.	
do.		Paris and Depart- ments.	
do.		do.	
Addition for the large Bigorne.		do.	
		do.	

TABULAR LIST OF THE ASSAY OFFICES IN THE DEPARTMENTS, DIVIDED
INTO NINE REGIONS, WITH THE CHARACTERISTIC SIGNS WHICH DIS-
TINGUISH THE PUNCHES OF EACH. USED 16 AUG. 1819—10 MAY, 1838.

DIVISIONS.	DEPARTMENTS.	BUREAUX.	Characteristic Signs.	
			Large Work.	Small Work.
I. NORD.	Nord	Lille	57	A
		Valenciennes	57*	C
		Dunkerque	57**	D
	Pas de Calais	Arras	60	E
		St. Omer	60*	H
	Somme	Amiens	75	J
	Aisne	Laon	2	M
	Seine Inférieure	Rouen	73	8
		Havre	73*	N
	Oise	Beauvais	58	T
	Eure	Evreux	25	V
	Eure et Loir	Chartres	26	X
	Seine et Oise	Versailles	72	Y
	Seine et Marne	Melun	71	✠
II. NORD-EST.	Ardennes	Mézières	7	A
	Meuse	Verdun	53	C
		Bar-le-Duc	53*	D
	Moselle	Metz	55	E
	Rhin (Bas)	Strasbourg	65	H
	Meurthe	Nanci	52	J
		Pont à Mousson	52*	M
		Lunéville	52**	8
	Vosges	Epinal	83	N
	Marne	Chàlons	49	T
		Reims	49*	V
	Marne (Haute)	Chaumont	50	X
		Langres	50*	Y
	Aube	Troyes	9	✠
III. EST.	Rhin (Haut)	Colmar	66	A
	Saône (Haute)	Vesoul	68	C
	Doubs	Besançon	23	D
		Montbeliard	23*	E
	Jura	Lons-le-Saulnier	37	H
	Côte d'Or	Dijon	19	J
	Saône et Loire	Macon	69	M
	Ain	Trévoux	1	8
	Isère	Grenoble	36	N
	Rhône	Lyon	67	T
IV. SUD-EST.	Var	Toulon	78	A
		Grasse	78*	C
	Bouches du Rhône	Marseille	12	D
		Aix	12*	E
		Arles	12**	H
	Gard	Nîmes	28	J
		Alais	28*	M
	Vaucluse	Avignon	79	8
	Alpes (Basses)	Digne	4	N
	Alpes (Hautes)	Gap	5	T
	Drôme	Valence	24	V
	Ardèche	Privas	6	X
	Loire (Haute)	Le Puy	41	Y
	Loire	St. Etienne	40	✠

TABULAR LIST OF THE ASSAY OFFICES, ETC.—*continued.*

DIVISIONS.	DEPARTMENTS.	BUREAUX.	Characteristic Signs. Large Work.	Small Work.
V. SUD.	Pyrénées Orientales	Perpignan	64	A
	Aude	Carcassonne	10	C
	Hérault	Montpellier	32	D
	Tarn	Castres	76	E
	Aveiron	Rodès	11	H
	Lozère	Mendes	46	J
	Lot	Cahors	44	M
	Cantal	Aurillac	14	8
	Corrèze	Tulle	18	N
VI. SUD-OUEST.	Ariège	Foix	8	A
	Garonne (Haute)	Toulouse	29	C
	Pyrénées (Hautes)	Tarbes	63	D
	Pyrénées (Basses)	{ Pau	62	E
		{ Baionne	62*	H
	Landes	Mont de Marsan	38	J
	Gers	Auch	30	M
	Tarn et Garonne	Montauban	77	8
	Lot et Garonne	Agen	45	N
	Gironde	Bordeaux	31	T
	Dordogne	Périgueux	22	V
VII. OUEST.	Charente	Angoulême	15	A
	Charente Inf.	{ La Rochelle	16	C
		{ Saintes	16*	D
	Vienne (Haute)	Limoges	82	E
	Vienne	Poitiers	81	H
	Vendée	Fontenai	80	J
	Deux Sèvres	Niort	74	M
	Loire Inférieure	Nantes	42	8
	Maine et Loire	Angers	47	N
	Indre et Loire	Tours	35	T
	Vienne	Châtellerault	..	✠
VIII. NORD-OUEST.	Finistère	Brest	27	A
	Morbihan	Vannes	54	C
	Côtes du Nord	St. Brieux	20	D
	Ille-et-Vilaine	{ Rennes	33	E
		{ St. Malo	33*	H
	Mayenne	Laval	51	J
	Sarthe	Le Mans	70	M
	Orne	Alençon	59	8
	Manche	{ St. Lô	48	N
		{ Valognes	48*	T
	Calvados	Caen	13	V
IX. CENTRE.	Puy de Dôme	Clermont	61	A
	Creuse	Guêret	21	C
	Allier	Moulins	3	D
	Indre	Châteauroux	34	E
	Loir et Cher	Blois	39	H
	Cher	Bourges	17	J
	Nièvre	Nevers	56	M
	Yonne	{ Auxerre	84	N
		{ Sens	84*	T
	Loiret	Orleans	43	8

TABLE OF STANDARD, ASSAY OFFICE, AND VERIFICATION MARKS FOR
PARIS AND THE DEPARTMENTS, MADE IN PURSUANCE OF AN ORDI-
NANCE OF 30 JUNE, 1835. USED FROM 10 MAY, 1838.

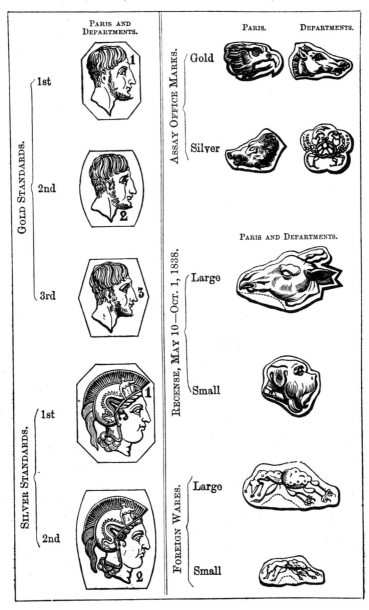

TABLE OF STANDARD, ASSAY OFFICE, AND VERIFICATION MARKS, ETC.
—*continued.*

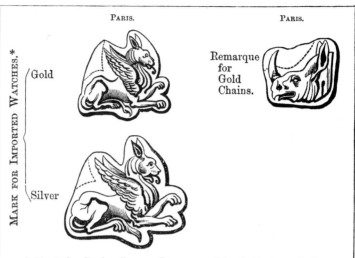

* Used in Paris, Lyons, Besançon, Montbéliard, and Lons-le-Saulnier.

NOTE.—In the figures of the above marks when used out of Paris the distinctive sign of one or other of the Assay Offices in the Departments would appear. There is no special mark to distinguish the punches used in Paris.

SPECIAL MARKS FOR WATCHES, MADE IN PURSUANCE OF AN ORDINANCE OF 19 SEPT. 1821.

NOTE.—The letter P signifies the Paris Office. The Departments had the number indicated for them in the Table (see p. 91) in use from 1819–1838.

ALPHABETICAL LIST OF THE DEPARTMENTS, SHOWING ALL THE ASSAY OFFICES THROUGHOUT FRANCE, AND THE CHARACTERISTIC SIGNS WHICH DISTINGUISH THE STANDARD AND ASSAY OFFICE PUNCHES IN EACH PLACE. USED FROM 10 MAY, 1838, IN CONJUNCTION WITH THE MARKS ON THE LAST PRECEDING TABLE (SEE P. 93).

No.	DEPT.	OFFICE.	Mark	No.	DEPT.	OFFICE.	Mark
1.	Ain	Trévoux	A	25.	Eure	Evreux	(mark)
2.	Aisne	Laon	(mark)	26.	Eure et Loir	Chartres	(mark)
3.	Allier	Moulins	(mark)	27.	Finistère	Brest	3
4.	Alpes (Basses)	Digne	(mark)	28.	Gard	Nimes	(mark)
5.	Alpes (Hautes)	Gap	C	29.	Garonne (Haute)	Toulouse	→
7.	Ardennes	Charleville	E	31.	Gironde	Bordeaux	θ
9.	Aube	Troyes	(mark)	32.	Hérault	Montpellier	(mark)
10.	Aude	Carcassonne	D	33.	Ile et Vilaine	Rennes	+
11.	Aveyron	Rodez	H	33.*	Ile et Vilaine	St. Malo	Z
12.	Bouches du Rhône	Marseilles	(mark)	35.	Indre et Loire	Tours	(mark)
13.	Calvados	Caen	(mark)	36.	Isère	Grenoble	(mark)
14.	Cantal	Aurillac	I	37.	Jura	Lons-le-Saulnier	N
15.	Charente	Angoulême	J	38.	Landes	Mont de Marsan	(triangle)
16.	Charente Inférieure	La Rochelle	K	39.	Loir et Cher	Blois	(mark)
16.*	Charente Inférieure	Saintes	L	40.	Loire	St. Etienne	(mark)
17.	Cher	Bourges	(mark)	41.	Loire (Haute)	Le Puy	(mark)
18.	Corrèze	Tulle	O	42.	Loire Inf.	Nantes	(mark)
19.	Côte d'Or	Dijon	(mark)	43.	Loiret	Orléans	(mark)
20.	Côtes du Nord	St. Brieux	S	44.	Lot	Cahors	(mark)
21.	Creuse	Guéret	T	45.	Lot et Garonne	Agen	(triangle)
22.	Dordogne	Perigueux	U	46.	Lozère	Mende	E
23.	Doubs	Besançon	W	47.	Maine et Loire	Angers	(mark)
23.*	Doubs	Montbéliard	(mark)	48.	Manche	St. Lo	(mark)
24.	Drôme	Valence	X				

ALPHABETICAL LIST OF DEPARTMENTS, ETC.—*continued*.

No.	Dept.	Office.		No.	Dept.	Office.	
48.*	Manche	Valognes		65.	Rhin (Bas)	Strasbourg	
49.	Marne	Chalons		66.	Rhin (Haut)	Colmar	
49.*	Marne	Reims		67.	Rhone	Lyon	
50.	Marne (Haute)	Chaumont		69.	Saone et Loire	Macon	
51.	Mayenne	Laval		70.	Sarthe	Le Mans	
52.	Meurthe	Nancy		72.	Seine In-férieure	Rouen	
53.	Meuse	Bar-le-Duc		72.*	Seine In-férieure	Havre	
53.*	Meuse	Verdun		73.	Seine et Marne	Melun	
54.	Morbihan	Vannes		74.	Seine et Oise	Versailles	
55.	Moselle	Metz		75.	Sèvres, Deux	Niort	
57.	Nord	Lille		76.	Somme	Amiens	
57.*	Nord	Dunkerque		77.	Tarn	Alby	
57.**	Nord	Valenciennes		79.	Var	Toulon	
58.	Oise	Beauvais		79.*	Var	Grasse	
59.	Orne	Alençon		80.	Vaucluse	Avignon	
60.	Pas de Calais	Arras		81.	Vendée	Fontenay	
60.*	Pas de Calais	St. Omer		82.	Vienne	Poitiers	
61.	Puy-de-Dôme	Clermont		82.*	Vienne	Chatellerault	
62.	Pyrénées (Basses)	Pau		83.	Vienne (Haute)	Limoges	
62*	Do.	Bayonne		84.	Vosges	Epinal	
63.	Pyrénées (Hautes)	Tarbes		85.	Yonne	Auxerre	
64.	Pyrénées Orientales	Perpignan					

Chased and embossed silver cup and cover, on three feet with three foliated handles. Barbedienne 1862. Victoria & Albert Museum.

INDEX.

——◆——

A.

PAGE

A, Paris mint letter 28, 41, 47, 62, 64
A A, Metz mint letter 63
Alphabetical date-letters, introduction of 20
Alphabetical letters, as Mint marks 28, 62
&, Aix mint mark 63
Apprentices, regulations as to 11
Argent le roy 6, 15
Arms of towns, anciently used as marks 50
    ,,   ,,   table of 56–61

B.

B, Rouen mint letter 62, 64
B P, Strasbourg mint letter 53
Ballin, Claude 26
    ,,   Jacques 35
Bigorne countermarks, how used 85
    ,,   ,,   table of 90
Blois, Ordinance of 19, 22
Boileau, Etienne, ancient regulations of 10
Bordeaux, goldsmiths of, and their marks 16, 62, 64
Borihls, what 17
Burgundy, standards used in 55

C.

C, Caen mint letter 62
Carat measure, when abolished 2
Cellini, Benvenuto 23, 26
Chains, remarque for gold 85, 94
Charge, poinçon de 28, 40, 52
Cock, a standard mark under the Republic 81, 86

PAGE

Coin, standards of French gold and silver 5, 6
,, weights of modern French 4
Common hall, punch of the 13, 39
Communities, lists and marks of provincial . . . 65, 91, 95
Countersign, first mention of 14
Crown, gratis mark 41

D.

D, mint letter of Lyons 62, 64
Date-letters, tables of Parisian 42–46
Décharge, poinçon de 28, 41
Delaulne, Etienne 24, 25
Deniers, a weight 2
Departments, marks used for the different 86–96
Destruction of plate at various epochs 27, 32
Divisional punches, of 1819 89
Droit de marque, impôsition of 27
Duty on plate 27, 41

E.

E, Tours mint letter 62
Esterlins, an ancient weight 2
E T, a mark for foreign wares 34, 81, 86, 87

F.

F, Angers mint letter 53
Fermier-général, marks used by the 41, 47, 52, 62
Fleur-de-lys, ancient Paris mark 13, 39
Fontainebleau, edict of 24
Foreign wares, marks used to distinguish . . . 34, 81, 86–88, 93

G.

G, Poitiers mint letter 62
Germain, Thomas 31
Gobelins, school of goldsmiths' art 26
Gold, mint price of standard 5
,, standards at various epochs for 4
,, value of various qualities of 5
Goldsmiths, lists of French 26, 30, 35
Gramme weights 2
,, ,, compared with Troy, etc. 3
Gratis, mark of 41
Gros, a weight 2

H.

PAGE

H, mint letter of La Rochelle 62
Hall-marks, origin of 12, 21

I.

I, Limoges mint letter 62
Insects, used as Bigorne marks 85, 90

J.

John, King of France, letters of 13

K.

K, Bordeaux mint letter 62, 64

L.

L, Bayonne mint letter 62
Lacroix's *Histoire de l'Orfèvrerie*, etc. 29, 35, 65
Le Roy, Pierre, code compiled by 32
Letters, initial and other, used as town marks 50
,, mint, used as plate marks 28, 41
,, tables of alphabetical year 42–46
Lily, an ancient Paris mark 13, 39
Limoges, the cradle of the goldsmiths' art 8
Lorraine, standards used in 55
Louis XIV., style of 29
,, XV., style of 31
,, XVI., style of 34
Louvre, school of the 26
Lyons, marks used at 62, 64

M.

M, Toulouse mint letter 62
Maker's mark, regulations respecting 14, 40
Marc weights 2
,, ,, compared with Troy, etc. 3
Marks, when first mentioned 12
Metric system, weights of the . . . .
Millesimal notation, introduction of 2
Mint letters as marks, use of 28, 41
Mint price for gold 5
Montpellier, records of 16, 21
,, ancient marks used at 17, 51

N.

PAGE

N, Montpellier mint letter 62

O.

O, Riom mint letter 62
Obole, an ancient weight 5
Or de touche 4, 15

P.

P, Dijon mint letter 62
P crowned, a Paris mark 36, 40
Paris, early mention of goldsmiths in 9
  ,, date-letters used at 42–46
  ,, mint letter for 28, 47, 62, 64
  ,, touch of 4
Philippe le Hardi, ordinances of 12
  ,, le Bel, ordinances of 12
Plate, destruction of, at various times 27, 32
Provincial marks, alphabetical lists of 56, 65, 95
  ,, towns, arms of 56
  ,, ,, marks used in 54
  ,, ,, mint letters of various 52, 62
Puy-en-Velay, the goldsmiths of 16, 50

Q.

Q, Perpignan mint letter 53

R.

R, Orleans mint letter 62
Recense, what 81, 82
Regency, style of the 30
Remarque, mark for gold chains 85, 94
Remedy, what 4, 15
Renaissance, effect of the 23
Republic, marks introduced under the 84
Rosnel, Pierre de 20
Rouen, the goldsmiths of 50
  ,, marks used at 51, 62, 64

S.

S, Chalons mint letter 62
Silver, value of various qualities of 7

PAGE

Solignac, the monks of 8
St. Eloi, patron of the goldsmiths 8
St. Martial, first patron of the craft 8
Standards of gold 4
,, provincial 55
,, silver 5
Sumptuary legislation 32

T.

T, Nantes mint letter 53
Tables of old Paris marks 42–49
,, ,, provincial marks 56, 62, 65
,, modern marks 86–96
Trinity, Hospital of the 33
Troy weight, compared with marcs, etc. 3
Troyes, the goldsmiths of 16, 50
Tours, the goldsmiths of 19
Town marks, lists of 56, 65

V.

V, an Amiens mint letter 53
Verification marks, when used 82

W.

W, a Lille mint letter 53
Wardens early mention of 12
,, their duties, etc. 21
Watches, marks for 94

X.

X, an Amiens and Soissons mint letter 62

Y.

Y, Bourges mint letter 63

Z.

Z, Grénoble mint letter 63